WHEN
THOU ART
CONVERTED

• • •

WHEN
THOU ART
CONVERTED

*Continuing Our Search
for Happiness*

• • •

M. RUSSELL BALLARD

DESERET
BOOK

SALT LAKE CITY, UTAH

Library of Congress Cataloging-in-Publication Data

Ballard, M. Russell, 1928-
    When thou art converted: continuing our search for happiness / M. Russell Ballard.
    p.   cm.
    Includes index.
    ISBN 1-57345-813-9 (hbk : alk. paper)
    1. Christian life—Mormon authors.   I. Title.
BX8656   .B35   2001
248.4'89332—dc21   2001004759

Printed in the United States of America   70582-6699
Phoenix Color Corporation, Hagerstown, MD

10   9   8   7   6   5   4   3   2   1

Contents

ACKNOWLEDGMENTS

First and foremost, I want to express my gratitude to my companion, Barbara. During these past fifty years together, she has taught me much about the basic concepts explored in this book. I hope that for both new and longtime members of The Church of Jesus Christ of Latter-day Saints a study of these principles will help anchor your testimonies firmly in gospel soil so that the challenges of life will not pull you away from what you know to be true. It is in continuing the search for a more thorough understanding of the gospel of Jesus Christ and in living its precepts that we are happiest.

While I gratefully acknowledge the contributions of many who have helped bring this manuscript to the point of publication, I would mention three by name: Joseph Walker, for the many hours spent in research and consultation; Sheri Dew and her colleagues at Deseret Book, for their encouragement and editorial expertise; and my secretary, Carolyn Hyde, for suggestions to improve the text as well for typing the manuscript and doing the necessary revisions

This book is not an official publication of the Church. I alone am responsible for its contents.

CONTINUING OUR SEARCH FOR HAPPINESS

I t was calm on the Sea of Tiberias that day. Uncommonly calm. That was probably a relief to Peter, who had seen and experienced more during the previous three years than most people experience in an entire lifetime. The past several weeks had been especially draining, first dragging him down to the greatest despair he had ever known when his Master, the Lord Jesus Christ, was crucified, and then launching him into a state of sublime joy just three days later when the Savior stood before him and the other Apostles as a resurrected being.

And now . . . what? Throughout His ministry, and especially during the last week, Jesus had spoken of His expectation that His followers would continue the work He had started. When He called and beckoned them to follow Him, He told them that He would make them "fishers of men" (Matthew 4:19). Just hours before He was betrayed and taken by Roman soldiers, He told His disciples, "Ye have not chosen me, but I have chosen you, and ordained you, that ye should go and bring forth fruit" (John 15:16). And to Peter He gave this very specific instruction: "When thou art converted, strengthen thy brethren" (Luke 22:32).

This last instruction had troubled Peter, just as I'm sure it would have troubled many of us in the same circumstance. Peter had left his fishing business to follow Christ. He had been at the Savior's side through most of His ministry, listening as He taught His gospel and watching as He performed mighty miracles. He had seen Him heal the sick, give sight to the blind and hearing to the deaf. He had probably been among those who gathered up baskets of food after Jesus had miraculously fed a great multitude with just a few loaves and fishes. He had been with Him on the Mount of Transfiguration, where Moses and Elias appeared to Christ to confer their priesthood keys upon Him. Peter had been the Lord's chief Apostle, a position Jesus Himself acknowledged when He referred to him as Cephas, His stone or rock: "Upon this rock," the Lord had said, referring to revelation through Peter as a prophet, "I will build my church" (Matthew 16:18).

And so when Jesus suggested that Peter would need to be thoroughly converted before he would be able to continue the work and ministry that Christ had started, the senior Apostle protested. "Lord," he said, "I am ready to go with thee, both into prison, and to death" (Luke 22:33).

But the Savior knew and understood that although Peter's heart was good and his intentions were noble and devout, there was yet something he lacked. I think there was great love and compassion in the Lord's voice when He calmly told Peter that "the cock shall not crow this day, before that thou shalt thrice deny that thou knowest me" (Luke 22:34). It wasn't that He doubted Peter or lacked confidence in him. In fact, the opposite is probably true. He loved Peter and trusted him implicitly, as future events would clearly manifest. But He knew and understood the human side of Peter—probably better than Peter knew and understood himself.

We know what happened next, of course. The Savior endured the most excruciatingly painful night ever endured by any man at any time in any place. He first went with a few of His disciples, including Peter, to the Garden of Gethsemane, where, in some extraordinary way beyond our comprehension, He took upon Himself the burden and pains of all our sins, all our guilt, and all our suffering. The sorrow and pain He felt was so great, so intense, and so overwhelming that it caused Him to bleed at every pore. At one point He even pled with His Father: "If thou be willing, remove this cup from me: nevertheless not my will, but thine, be done" (Luke 22:42).

And where was Peter while the most momentous event in the entire history of mankind was taking place? He and two of his brethren, James and John, were just a few yards away from the Savior in another part of the garden—asleep.

"What, could ye not watch with me one hour?" the Lord asked Peter, chiding him gently. And then He offered this great insight into the soul of His friend and follower: "The spirit indeed is willing, but the flesh is weak" (Matthew 26:40–41).

That same scenario played itself out again in different ways during the ensuing hours, as Jesus was betrayed, captured, questioned, ridiculed, beaten, spat upon, and scourged. Peter was nearby—waiting, watching, wondering in the shadows. Three times he was questioned about his association with Christ. Three times he denied knowing Him, each time more vehemently. At one point, Matthew records, he began "to curse and to swear, saying, I know not the man" (Matthew 26:74). When at last the morning came and the rooster crowed its welcome to the sun, "Peter remembered the word of Jesus, which said unto him, Before the cock crow, thou shalt deny me thrice. And he went out, and wept bitterly" (Matthew 26:75).

Clearly, Peter was not yet ready to continue the Savior's work and ministry. Nor did the events of the next few days, including the Lord's agonizing death on the cross at Calvary and His glorious emergence from the tomb three days later, fully prepare him to "strengthen [his] brethren." For even after having been twice visited and taught by the resurrected Christ, when left to himself and to his own devices, Peter and his friends returned to the sea to be fishers of fish, not of men.

And so it was that Jesus found Peter and several others of His disciples at the Sea of Tiberias on that calm spring morning. It had been a long and unsuccessful night of fishing, and they were hauling their heavy nets into the boat when they saw the figure of a lone, unrecognized man on the shore.

"Children," He called to them from the shore, "have ye any meat?"

"No," was their terse reply. I can just hear the tone of their voice in that simple, one-word response, can't you? As a fisherman who has returned home empty-handed on more than one occasion, I'm well acquainted with that tone—and that feeling. When you come home with a creel full of fish, you're talkative and enthusiastic. When the creel is empty, however, you're much more inclined toward one-word answers—like "no."

"Cast the net on the right side of the ship," He told them, "and ye shall find."

It is interesting to me that even though at the time they didn't know who was giving them fishing advice, they did just as He told them to do. John records, "They cast therefore, and now they were not able to draw it for the multitude of fishes" (John 21:5-6). All night they had labored on the Sea of Tiberias, casting out their nets and pulling them in, time after backbreaking time, and they had caught nothing. Now, after just a word from a stranger on the shore, they cast their nets once more and pulled in more fish than they could handle. It seemed almost . . . miraculous.

That could only mean one thing, as far as John was concerned: "It is the Lord" (John 21:7).

Upon hearing that Christ was on the shore, Peter leapt into the sea and swam to meet Him. (Whatever it was Peter lacked, it certainly wasn't enthusiasm, loyalty, or love for the Lord.) Once the others joined them on shore, they sat together around a fire and ate a simple meal of bread and fish that the Savior had prepared for them. With their nets and stomachs full, they were ready to receive more training from the Master Teacher. Note how in the following verses Christ uses the teaching technique of repetition to help Peter understand his new calling and assignment in this life:

"So when they had dined, Jesus saith to Simon Peter, Simon, son of Jonas, lovest thou me more than these [meaning the fish]? He saith unto him, Yea, Lord; thou knowest that I love thee. He saith unto him, Feed my lambs.

"He saith to him again the second time, Simon, son of Jonas, lovest thou me? He saith unto him, Yea, Lord; thou knowest that I love thee. He saith unto him, Feed my sheep.

"He saith unto him the third time, Simon, son of Jonas, lovest thou me? Peter was grieved because he said unto him the third time, Lovest thou me? And he said unto him, Lord, thou knowest all things; thou knowest that I love thee. Jesus saith unto him, Feed my sheep" (John 21:15-17).

Do you think the Savior was trying to make a point to Peter? Over and over and over He taught him: Feed my sheep. Feed my lambs. Build my kingdom. Continue my work. "For I have given you an example," He told His disciples several days earlier, "that ye should do as I have done to you" (John 13:15).

There followed a period of training and education, during which the Lord prepared His disciples for the important new roles they would have to play in His earthly kingdom, now that He no longer would dwell among them. "Go ye therefore, and teach all nations," He instructed them, "baptizing them in the name of the Father, and of the Son, and of the Holy Ghost: teaching them to observe all things whatsoever I have commanded you: and, lo, I am with you alway, even unto the end of the world" (Matthew 28:19-20).

This time the lesson seemed to stick with Peter and the

others, especially after the day of Pentecost, when they were blessed with the gift of the Holy Ghost. Empowered with priesthood authority, enlightened by divine truth taught by the source of all light and truth, and infused with the heart-changing spiritual witness of the Holy Ghost, Peter became the rock-solid Church leader that Christ had promised he would one day be. Once he was truly converted, he wore out his life strengthening his brethren and sisters in the gospel and continuing the work of his Lord and Savior, Jesus Christ.

WHAT DO WE DO NOW?

At some point in our lives, we arrive at a place where we, like Peter, must ask ourselves, What do we do now? Usually at that point we recognize we have been given blessings from God: blessings of health and strength, blessings of prosperity, blessings of physical capability, blessings of knowledge, wisdom, insight, or inspiration. Perhaps we have worked to enlarge and expand those gifts; or perhaps, as with some, it may appear we have worked to hide them. My experience indicates that real success in this life—both temporally and spiritually—depends upon the decisions we make at these moral crossroads. Where are we going to go? What are we going to do? How do we take what we have received and move forward with it?

A few years ago, in a book called *Our Search for Happiness: An Invitation to Understand The Church of Jesus Christ of Latter-day Saints,* I tried to explain the basic teachings and beliefs of the Church in a clear and inoffensive way. My greatest hope was that those who read the book would receive from it enhanced understanding of what it means to be a member of The Church of Jesus Christ of Latter-day Saints. It wasn't an attempt at persuasion or conversion, although I have heard from many who joined the Church after reading the book as part of their introduction to the gospel. I wanted people to know what we believe and, to some extent, understand why we do what we do and why we feel what we feel.

But now . . . what? Now that the basics have been presented and are understood to one degree or another, what's next? Where do we go from here? What do we do now?

This book is an attempt to help us take the next logical step. Like Peter, we have already learned much in our personal search for happiness. Now it is time to become truly converted, to experience what the Book of Mormon prophet Alma called a "mighty change in your hearts" (Alma 5:14). Once we are converted, we can reach out to our "brethren"—our families, friends and associates—to make a positive difference in the world around us. And what better time to begin that process than right now, during the first years of a new millennium?

To that end, I am recommending within these pages eleven keys that I believe will help us as we continue our search for happiness and peace during these challenging and yet exhilarating times. They include the following:

- Building and strengthening our testimony
- Recognizing our eternal identity as a child of God
- Cultivating balance in living
- Learning to recognize and respond to the Spirit
- Learning the lessons of the past
- Standing for truth and righteousness
- Serving others
- Honoring the priesthood
- Honoring womanhood
- Following the prophet
- Focusing on the family

IS IT WORTH IT?

Before we get started, one introductory question deserves our attention. It is the same question you may have asked yourself when you were going through the process of buying your first car or your first home or making some other significant financial investment. It's a question that my wife, Barbara, and I struggled with when we bought our first home. We spent a long time looking all over the valley for a home we could afford and that would meet our needs. When we finally found a house that looked perfect, I went to my father for counsel. He went with us and looked at the home we had chosen. It appeared that he was pleased with what he was seeing, but he didn't voice an opinion one way or the other. Finally, he asked me just one question: "Is it worth it?"

We knew it would be a sacrifice. Although the mortgage payment of sixty-seven dollars a month was, by today's standards, very small, at the time it seemed a great deal of money and a huge monthly commitment of our income. The house was small but just right to get started, and it was in a neighborhood consisting primarily of young married couples. Barbara and I both felt it would be a good place to raise our family.

"It's worth it, Dad," I said. "Whatever it takes, it's worth it."

And you know what? Even though we had to scrimp a little at first, it was worth it.

"Is it worth it?" isn't just a question we must answer with regard to financial decision making, although it certainly is an important issue in that forum. Every day we wrestle with this same question in a variety of different areas and concerns. College students struggling to make their way through school while working full-time and starting their family ask it. Parents trying to teach their children such life-changing values as faith, virtue, and honesty ask it. Sunday School teachers working and praying to hold the attention of uninterested teenagers ask it. Athletes running their fiftieth wind sprint in a row ask it. Business owners working their thirty-third consecutive sixteen-hour day ask it. Police officers arresting a career criminal for the seventh time ask it. We all ask it at least occasionally and sometimes daily. I would hope that we are wise enough to realize that we can excel, we can reach the top, we can be the very best in any field or endeavor—if we are willing to pay the price. But in order to be great in whatever we attempt to do in life, we have to decide in advance that it is indeed worth it.

The same question can be asked of our eternal goals and priorities. Although salvation (immortality with a resurrected body) is available to all mankind through the loving grace of the Lord Jesus Christ, exaltation (life eternal in the highest degree of the celestial kingdom, the place where God and Christ dwell) requires great faith and service on our part. We must sacrifice. We must be obedient. We must repent of our sins and work to take full advantage of the remarkable possibilities afforded to all mankind through the Atonement of Christ. It isn't easy. No one ever said that it would be. The question for us to consider is, Is it worth it?

As sons and daughters of God, we have a great challenge, a great work to do, and a great destiny. Consider these impressive words from the Doctrine and Covenants:

"And again we bear record—for we saw and heard, and this is the testimony of the gospel of Christ concerning them who shall come forth in the resurrection of the just—they are they who received the testimony of Jesus, and believed on his name and were baptized after the manner of his burial, being buried in the water in his name, and this according to the commandment which he has given" (D&C 76:50-51).

Like many Church members, I was baptized at the age of eight. As I read that scripture now and contemplate the decision I made then to be baptized, I conclude that I really did not make much of a decision on that day. My mother and father, to whom I am grateful, felt that I should be baptized. I can remember my interview with the bishop, and I remember the coaching from my mother before the interview. She told me, "Now, the bishop is going to ask you why you want to be baptized." I listened with great interest to hear the answer I should give the bishop. She also told me I would be asked about receiving the Holy Ghost and being confirmed. She taught me why that was important. I went to my interview and passed it with flying colors; all of the questions were exactly as my mother had said they would be, and I gave all the right answers. But I really did not make much of a decision.

Those who choose to join the Church later in life have to ponder the question of whether or not to be baptized. But all of us, no matter the age at which we were baptized, have to deal with the next verse in this passage of scripture every single day, if not every minute, of our lives. The Lord said, "By keeping the commandments they might be washed and cleansed from all their sins, and receive the Holy Spirit by the laying on of the hands of him who is ordained and sealed unto this power" (D&C 76:52).

Think about that for a moment in the context of the question at hand: "Is it worth it?" Is it worth keeping all of the commandments? Is it worth being morally clean? Is it worth living the Word of Wisdom? Is it worth being honest? Is it worth paying your tithes and offerings? Is it worth serving faithfully wherever you are called?

Each moment of each day we are faced with decisions based on the evaluation system we have developed through training in our homes and in the Church. The guidelines are clear, and our vision should be riveted on the long-range goal of qualifying to inherit the highest degree of glory in the celestial kingdom. I do not believe for a minute that simply wanting that great and glorious blessing will bring it to us unless we are willing to repent as necessary and strive always to keep the commandments.

And now let us think about the next verse in Doctrine and Covenants 76: "And who overcome by faith, and are sealed by the Holy Spirit of promise, which the Father sheds forth upon all those who are just and true" (v. 53).

It is possible to fool your mother and your father. It is even possible to fool your bishop and your stake president. But you cannot fool the Holy Ghost. Live your life in such a way that the Holy Spirit, or the Holy Ghost, can testify to the Father on your behalf that you have in very deed been just and true in keeping all of the commandments. The only safe course is to strive earnestly to keep the commandments every day and to repent of any sins, always remembering that the ultimate, long-range, eternal goal is the celestial kingdom.

IT IS WORTH IT!

Is that kind of commitment worth it? According to the Doctrine and Covenants, those who make that commitment and follow through on it "are they into whose hands the Father has given all things" (D&C 76:55).

Do you understand the extraordinary significance of that simple statement of scriptural fact? Consider it in the context of the question before us: "Is it worth it?" Those who keep the commandments, who are just and true, are they of whom the Holy Ghost can truly testify before the Father, "They are they who have kept the commandments and into whose hands the Father has given all things."

Ponder that. Let that idea crystallize in your heart and your soul. Think about what is being promised and who is promising it. Heavenly Father, through His great and exalted understanding and mastery of the holy priesthood and with His beloved Son, Jesus Christ, organized this world on which we live. Matter unorganized was organized into this glorious world upon which you and I dwell. By the power of the priesthood authority of Almighty God, daylight was separated from darkness and the land from the sea; the fishes were placed in the sea and the fowls in the air. Everything that exists in this world—everything!—was created by, through, and of Him. There is nothing good that exists without His will and pleasure. When I contemplate the creation process and realize that the Father promises to all His sons and daughters who are willing to pay the price of keeping His commandments that He will give them all that He has—everything!—I feel that it is indeed worth the price.

"Wherefore," the passage continues, "as it is written, they are gods, even the sons of God" (D&C 76:58).

Oh, if we could only begin to understand what that really means! If we could just place that priority properly in our lives and live up to it, we would never have any difficulty making the right decisions. We would always have tucked in the back of our minds this eternal reality: "It is worth it." Therefore, we would not compromise. We would not look for shortcuts. We would pay any price, under any circumstances, because we know more surely than we know anything that it is worth it.

Not only does Heavenly Father promise us all that He has but He also promises that those who are willing to pay the price of true discipleship "shall dwell in the presence of God and his Christ forever and ever" (D&C 76:62).

Is that where you want to go? Is that where you want to be? I know it is where I want to be. And I know it will be worth it. Elder Melvin J. Ballard, my grandfather, recorded as his testimony one of the great witnesses of this generation. In stunning vision, he knelt in the presence of the Savior of this world and was embraced by Him and blessed by Him. In his testimony before the Quorum of the Twelve Apostles and the First Presidency in the Salt Lake Temple on 9 January 1919, he said: "Oh! If I could live worthy, though it would require four-score years, so that in the end when I have finished I could go into His presence and receive the feeling that I then had in His presence, I would give everything that I am and ever hope to be!" (in Ballard, *Melvin J. Ballard*, 66).

That is where we are talking about trying to go. We are trying to qualify for that blessing and honor.

Is it worth it? It most certainly is.

Continuing in Doctrine and Covenants 76: "These are they whose bodies are celestial, whose glory is that of the sun, even the glory of God, the highest of all, whose glory the sun of the firmament is written of as being typical" (v. 70).

"And thus we saw the glory of the celestial, which excels in all things—where God, even the Father, reigns upon his throne forever and ever" (v. 92).

"And he makes them equal in power, and in might, and in dominion. And the glory of the celestial is one, even as the glory of the sun is one" (vv. 95-96).

That is a great objective—almost overwhelming in its scope and magnitude. But it is attainable if we are willing to pay the price.

A little later in the Doctrine and Covenants, the Lord makes this promise to those who faithfully obtain and magnify priesthood offices (and who make and keep sacred priesthood covenants in the temple):

"They become the sons of Moses and of Aaron and the seed of Abraham, and the church and kingdom, and the elect of God. And also all they who receive this priesthood receive me, saith the Lord; for he that receiveth my servants receiveth me; and he that receiveth me receiveth my Father; and he that receiveth my Father receiveth my Father's kingdom; therefore all that my Father hath shall be given unto him" (D&C 84:34-38).

Is it worth it? Is it worth giving all the attention and all the energy of which we are capable for the building of God's great kingdom here upon the earth in exchange for "all that my Father hath"? Yes, it is!

SAFETY IN OBEDIENCE

"But," you might say, "it's hard, Brother Ballard. There are so many things out there that I have to conquer." Heavenly Father knows that; He knows that it is difficult. That is why He gave us commandments to follow. They are not there to limit our agency or to complicate our lives. They are given to us because our Heavenly Father loves us and wants to provide a safe, secure road we can travel that will bring us home to Him.

As Elder Richard L. Evans wrote: "Our Father in heaven is not an umpire who is trying to count us out. He is not a competitor who is trying to outsmart us. He is not a prosecutor who is trying to convict us. He is a Loving Father who wants our happiness and eternal progress and everlasting opportunity and glorious accomplishment, and who will help us all he can if we will but give him, in our lives, the opportunity to do so with obedience and humility and faith and patience" (Conference Report, October 1956, 101).

Therefore, do not tamper with the commandments. Do not think that you are above them, or that they don't apply to you, or that you will live them later when you have more time and inclination for such things, or that there will be plenty of time to repent later. Just live them—right now, today—because living God's commandments is right. There is safety in it. It is all that Heavenly Father asks of us in exchange for all that He is waiting—yearning—to give to us as His children.

It is worth it!

The importance of such obedience came home hard for me soon after I was called to be a General Authority. President Ezra Taft Benson telephoned to assign me to speak at a funeral service for a missionary who had lost his life in the mission field. I believe I felt more anxiety in approaching that assignment than I had felt in preparing to speak in general conference. During the course of my preparation, I called the young man's mission president and asked, "What kind of an elder was he?"

"Outstanding," the president said. "He could have been given any assignment in our mission, and I knew he would have performed well and faithfully. Brother Ballard, I just didn't have any finer missionary than this young man."

What a thrill it was to know that that missionary was living worthy of the celestial kingdom on his mission and to be able to assure his family that all was well with their son. I am sure he did not expect to be called home while serving a mission. I am sure he did not expect that accident to occur. But it happened. He was alive and well in the morning and gone in the afternoon. Gone where? Back to the presence of our Father in Heaven, to inherit all that the Father has. Do you think it was worth it to him to be an obedient, faithful missionary? Infinitely so.

CONTINUING OUR SEARCH FOR HAPPINESS

This, then, is where we find ourselves as we continue our personal search for happiness and peace. We have received knowledge and insight, information and inspiration. As discussed in *Our Search for Happiness,* we know that the Lord restored His Church through the Prophet Joseph Smith. We know the way the priesthood was restored, how the Book of Mormon was translated, how the ordinances of salvation were reestablished upon the earth. We know and understand the basics. Our feet are on the path. We just need to know in which direction to walk. It is my hope that the following pages will provide some of that direction. Some of what you read here will be new to you; most of it will not. When it comes right down to it, there isn't a lot that can be added to the time-honored principles of spiritual growth: study, pray, obey—and work.

We must work to continue our search. Just as Peter had to learn how to continue in the work that Christ had for him to do, we must learn what is expected of us as we continue to grow as faithful followers of the Lord Jesus Christ. That doesn't necessarily mean that our callings or responsibilities in the kingdom will become greater or more intense. It only means that we will continue to grow in knowledge and understanding, in obedience and commitment, in faith, in hope, in charity. As the Lord taught through the Prophet Joseph Smith, "He that receiveth light, and continueth in God, receiveth more light; and that light groweth brighter and brighter until the perfect day" (D&C 50:24).

And at that day, I promise you, it will be worth it.

CHAPTER 1

BUILDING AND STRENGTHENING OUR TESTIMONY

Have you ever watched a large ship weigh anchor? It is a fascinating thing to see and hear the massive links of chain screeching against the metal bow of the ship as the anchor is lowered or raised. The metal shanks of the anchor chain are incredibly heavy, but their weight is slight when compared to the total weight of the ship. Still, when placed properly, an anchor can a keep a giant ship from drifting away on the tides or currents. Even in storm-tossed seas, it can help keep a ship safely facing into the wind.

Like ships, we need anchors in our lives, spiritual anchors to help us remain steadfast and avoid drifting into the sea of temptation and sin. Faith in God and His Son, the Lord Jesus Christ, is the main anchor we must have in our lives to hold us fast during the times of social turbulence and wickedness that seem to be everywhere today. For it to provide a meaningful and effective anchor that will hold us fast, our faith must be centered in Jesus Christ, His life and His Atonement, and in the restoration of His gospel to the earth in the last days.

Repeatedly, when asked by reporters to explain the dramatic growth of the Church, President Gordon B. Hinkley has said that the gospel of Jesus Christ gives men and women an anchor in a world of shifting tides and values. I couldn't agree more.

Not too long ago I spoke to a group of prospective missionaries. Many of those young men and women had already decided to serve a full-time mission, but others were not certain they should—or would—accept a call to serve. You might think I would be inclined to push a little bit, to see if I could persuade them to make that important commitment to serve a full-time mission. But as significant as that decision is in the life of young Latter-day Saints everywhere, there is an even more important decision that they must make, and that's the decision upon which I focused with those young people. I told them they did not have to decide that night whether or not to go on a mission; however, I told them, they needed to decide whether or not Joseph Smith knelt in the presence of God the Father and His Son, Jesus Christ, "on the morning of a beautiful, clear day, early in the spring of eighteen hundred and twenty" (Joseph Smith–History 1:14).

I read to them Joseph Smith's own account of the event:

"After I had retired to the place where I had previously designed to go, having looked around me, and finding myself alone, I kneeled down and began to offer up the desires of my heart to God. I had scarcely done so, when immediately I was seized upon by some power which entirely overcame me, and had such an astonishing influence over me as to bind my tongue so that I could not speak. Thick darkness gathered around me, and it seemed to me for a time as if I were doomed to sudden destruction.

"But, exerting all my powers to call upon God to deliver me out of the power of this enemy which had seized upon me, and at the very moment when I was ready to sink into despair and abandon myself to destruction—not to an imaginary ruin, but to the power of some actual being from the unseen world, who had such marvelous power as I had never before felt in any being—just at this moment of great alarm, I saw a pillar of light exactly over my head, above the brightness of the sun, which descended gradually until it fell upon me.

"It no sooner appeared than I found myself delivered from the enemy which held me bound. When the light rested upon me I saw two Personages, whose brightness and glory defy all description, standing above me in the air. One of them spake unto me, calling me by name and said, pointing to the other— *This is My Beloved Son. Hear Him!*" (Joseph Smith-History 1:15-17).

If this truly happened to Joseph Smith—and I testify to you with all the power of my soul that it did—then the question of whether or not these prospective missionaries should serve a mission pretty much takes care of itself, doesn't it? Knowing, really knowing, that Heavenly Father and His Beloved Son, Jesus Christ, appeared to and spoke with Joseph Smith as he said they did, kindles a strong desire to serve God and His Holy Son to the very best of one's ability.

Nothing is more remarkable or important in this life than to know that God our Eternal Father and His Son, Jesus Christ, have spoken again from the heavens and have called prophets and Apostles to teach the fulness of the everlasting gospel once again upon the earth. That is a glorious thing to know. When you know it, that knowledge profoundly affects your life. It influences every major decision you make. It changes the course of your life to a safer one because it provides an anchor that helps to hold you fast to the teachings of the gospel despite the evil influences all around that entice you to drift toward sin and transgression.

I make the same argument for the restoration of the Aaronic Priesthood through John the Baptist and the Melchizedek Priesthood through Peter, James, and John. Let's be very plain about this: either the priesthood of God has been restored, or it has not. When you know that it has, you have secured your spiritual anchor even more firmly against the turbulence and storms of life.

Similarly, either the Book of Mormon is the word of God and is another testament of Jesus Christ, or it is not. Either it is the record of the Lord's dealings with the people on the American continent from 600 B.C. to A.D. 421, translated by Joseph Smith under divine guidance, or it is not. The issue is that simple and that profound. If the Book of Mormon is, in fact, the word of God—as I testify that it is—then the question of whether or not we should apply its principles and teachings in our own lives is already decided, isn't it?

The same simple test applies to our living prophets and Apostles today. Either they are prophets of God in every sense, in every way, or they are not. It really is no more complicated than that. If we know these things to be true, there should be no question about how we should live and what we should do with our lives. If we know that we are anchored to "the only true and living church upon the face of the whole earth" (D&C 1:30), our course is clear. What a marvelous blessing it is to know this.

Most importantly, either Jesus is the Christ, or He isn't. Either He was Jehovah of the Old Testament, or He wasn't. Either He wrought the Atonement—which blesses us with peace, power, and the privilege of repentance—or He didn't. I testify that He is who He says He is and that He will do what He said He would do.

MOVING GOD-WARD

But how do we find out for ourselves if these things are true? As with so many things in life, it all begins with the first principle of the gospel: faith in the Lord Jesus Christ (Article of Faith 4). Because we have an anchor of faith in the Lord Jesus Christ, we understand that we must pray to receive a personal testimony. We understand that the Holy Ghost "shall teach you all things, and bring all things to your remembrance" (John 14:26). When we know and live these simple truths, they become a spiritual anchor to help us keep our own lives from being "tossed to and fro, and carried about with every wind of doctrine" (Ephesians 4:14). Becoming firmly grounded in these simple truths and focusing our attention on the lessons of eternity will keep us moving in the right direction at all times and in all situations, no matter which way the winds of worldly trends may be blowing.

Ella Wheeler Wilcox observed while she was a passenger on a steamship watching one ship sail west and another east in the same wind:

> One ship drives east and another west
> With the selfsame winds that blow.
> 'Tis the set of the sails
> And not the gales
> Which tells us the way to go.
>
> Like the winds of the sea are the ways of fate,
> As we voyage along through life:
> 'Tis the set of a soul
> That decides the goal,
> And not the calm or the strife.
>
> ("The Winds of Fate")

The most important thing we can learn in this life is how to set our personal sails so that no matter which way the wind blows, we continue moving God-ward. As we do that, everything else in our lives comes into sharper focus, and our faith in Christ becomes a solid anchor of assurance and discipleship.

Our English word disciple comes from the Latin discipulus; it means "to learn or to know." Many people think that being a disciple means simply to follow, with an unfortunate connotation of following blindly. Becoming a true disciple of Jesus

Christ is nothing of the sort! It requires us to learn and to know Jesus Christ, to study the principles of truth for ourselves and to receive answers; in other words, to receive knowledge through personal revelation. Once we have knowledge of the simple principles of the Restoration, coupled with a deep and abiding faith in the truths we are yet learning, we become true disciples of Jesus Christ and not simply followers.

Remember these words from the prophet Nephi: "Wherefore, ye must press forward with a steadfastness in Christ, having a perfect brightness of hope, and a love of God and of all men. Wherefore, if ye shall press forward, feasting upon the word of Christ, and endure to the end, behold, thus saith the Father: Ye shall have eternal life" (2 Nephi 31:20).

Every prophet, including those of the Old Testament, the New Testament, the Book of Mormon, and the Restoration, has had to go through the process of becoming a true disciple by coming to an unshakable knowledge of Christ. Each one has had to ask himself—just as I have asked you to ask yourself—"Is Jesus Christ the Son of God, our Eternal Father? Does He live? Does He preside over His Church today?"

The sure knowledge that Jesus Christ is the Savior and Redeemer of the world provided the courage for Shadrach, Meshach, and Abed-nego to enter a fiery furnace without fear. Abinadi's knowledge of Christ gave him the power to testify of Christ while being burned to death by King Noah and his wicked priests. The same knowledge that Christ lives gave Nephi the power to endure the incessant persecutions of his brothers. Having come to know Christ, Elijah had the power to command fire to consume his soggy altar while the priests of Baal watched in awe. One-time antagonist Saul of Tarsus became a stalwart Apostle once he knew of Christ's divinity and of His divinely appointed mission. An absolute conviction that Jesus Christ is the Messiah gave Samuel the Lamanite the courage to stand on the city wall and bear testimony to the wicked Nephites and to receive protection from their arrows and stones. The brother of Jared was even able to move the mountain Zerin because he knew in his heart of hearts that Jesus Christ is the Son of the living God. And certainly Joseph Smith left a powerful witness to the world of the reality of God the Father and of His Son:

"I had actually seen a light, and in the midst of that light I saw two Personages, and they did in reality speak to me; and though I was hated and persecuted for saying that I had seen a vision, yet it was true; and while they were persecuting me, reviling me, and speaking all manner of evil against me falsely for so saying, I was led to say in my heart: Why persecute me for telling the truth? I have actually seen a vision; and who am I that I can withstand God, or why does the world think to make me deny what I have actually seen? For I had seen a vision; I knew it, and I knew that God knew it, and I could not deny it, neither dared I do it; at least I knew that by so doing I would offend God, and come under condemnation" (Joseph Smith-History 1:25).

The scriptures are filled with righteous acts and testimonies of men and women who came to know for themselves that Jesus is the Christ. That same sure testimony of Jesus can be yours because the gospel has been restored in its fulness in the last days. Testimony and knowledge come as a result of your personal faith and prayers, even if at first you can only muster the desire to believe. Ask your Heavenly Father to bless you with faith and courage, as did the father who brought his son to the Lord to be healed, saying:

"If thou canst do any thing, have compassion on us, and help us. Jesus said unto him, If thou canst believe, all things are possible to him that believeth. And straightway the father of the child cried out, and said with tears, Lord, I believe; help thou mine unbelief" (Mark 9:22-24).

He can and will help you endure any challenges you may face. He will help you overcome loneliness, feelings of desperation, and hopelessness. He will help you find a way to resolve setbacks of a personal, emotional, financial, and even spiritual nature. He will strengthen you when you are simply feeling overwhelmed by all the demands for your time and attention. He will give you the ability to serve faithfully in every assignment you receive from your Church leaders. Your faith and your knowledge of the restoration of the gospel will give you the strength to be faithful and true to the covenants you have made with the Lord and to share your strengths and talents gladly to build up the kingdom of God here on the earth. Your testimony of Jesus Christ is the most important anchor you can have to help hold you, steadfast and immovable, to principles of righteousness, regardless of the challenges and temptations that may come in the future.

Moroni explained this principle when he spoke of the prophet Ether, who "could not be restrained because of the Spirit of the Lord which was in him. For he did cry from the morning, even until the going down of the sun, exhorting the people to believe in God unto repentance lest they should be destroyed, saying unto them that by faith all things are fulfilled—wherefore, whoso believeth in God might with surety hope for a better world, yea, even a place at the right hand of God, which hope cometh of faith, maketh an anchor to the souls of men, which would make them sure and steadfast, always abounding in good works, being led to glorify God" (Ether 12:2–4).

The principle is clear. We believe, we hope, we have faith, we act upon that faith by "abounding in good works," and we have an attitude of glorifying God. Then, at the end of our mortal journey through the seas of life, we shall, indeed, have a place at the right hand of God.

CHAPTER 2

RECOGNIZING OUR ETERNAL IDENTITY AS A CHILD OF GOD

L et's step back and take a look at the idea of a spiritual anchor from a little broader perspective. We live in a world where many are lost because they do not have a spiritual anchor of any kind to hold them secure when buffeted by the worldly waves and wind. The Prophet Joseph Smith taught that "there are many yet on the earth among all sects, parties, and denominations, who are blinded by the subtle craftiness of men, whereby they lie in wait to deceive, and who are only kept from the truth because they know not where to find it" (D&C 123:12).

Those of our Father's children who know that through Joseph Smith the fulness of the gospel of Jesus Christ has been restored are most blessed. With this precious knowledge comes a duty to prepare ourselves spiritually to serve God and our fellowmen. We can be the antidote to much of the moral decline in America and the world! We who have testimonies of the restored gospel, we who know the true nature of God, we who have the light of the Holy Ghost within us can be a spiritual lighthouse to the people of the world.

The Savior made this statement in the book of John: "I am

come a light into the world, that whosoever believeth on me should not abide in darkness" (John 12:46). Darkness is all about us. As a result of being exposed to the problems that exist in the world through my assignments in many countries, I have an overwhelming concern for the darkness that is in the lives of most of our Father's children.

Darkness is referred to in the scriptures as being evil, with the primary source of darkness being the devil, or Satan. He has the power to lead people into darkness, and his every effort is designed to shut them off, if he can, from the light and truth of the gospel of Jesus Christ, thus destroying souls by darkness. Said the Savior: "Yet a little while is the light with you. Walk while ye have the light, lest darkness come upon you: for he that walketh in darkness knoweth not whither he goeth. While ye have light, believe in the light, that ye may be the children of light" (John 12:35–36). That was an admonition given by the Son of God in His early ministry to those who were closely connected with Him.

I came to a better understanding of what it means to have the light of the gospel of Jesus Christ as our companion and guide when I was assigned to supervise Church work in the southeastern part of the United States. In that capacity I had the great opportunity to meet with missionaries in zone conferences. After one such zone conference in the South Carolina Columbia Mission, an elder wrote to me about an experience he and his companion had. I suppose this is not unlike experiences many missionary companionships have shared:

"We were working in the poorer section of a town without much success," the companion recounted. "The last family on the street invited us into their home. It was a run-down house with a wooden porch that had a few boards missing from it, hard wooden floors, a pot-bellied stove for warmth, and two bedrooms where a father and mother and five children slept on homemade cots. In general it was a place I had only read about in such novels as *Huckleberry Finn,* by Mark Twain.

"It was a hot, sultry afternoon, and it was time to head back to our apartment for dinner and then go on exchanges with ward members in the evening," the missionary continued. "I was thinking more about the evening's coming activities than I was about this family. After all, we had been in dozens of such homes with no apparent success.

"At the conclusion of the discussion with the family, I was surprised that we were invited back for a visit a few nights later. As my companion and I were walking down the street after our meeting, he indicated how strongly he felt about the family and expressed his confidence that we could baptize them. Those words stuck with me until our next meeting with the family, when I made sure that I was more spiritually in tune than I had been at the first meeting. Within a month, the family was living the Word of Wisdom and paying their tithing. My companion and I baptized and confirmed them."

This young missionary reminded me that the only thing that matters is the testimony that Jesus is the Christ, the son of the living God, that He is the source of all light, that by His light we can walk fearlessly with head held high and bring souls home to God—including our own. That's why we do what we do. That's why we have the Church. That's why we have wards, stakes, and missions. We have them for only one purpose, when all is said and done, and God has stated what that purpose is: "This is my work and my glory—to bring to pass the immortality and eternal life of man" (Moses 1:39). We seek to qualify some-day to walk into His sacred presence. We seek to have our lives sanctified, purified, and cleansed to the point where we can be found worthy to walk into the presence of our heavenly parents and Jesus Christ, our Savior and our Redeemer.

I don't believe there is any question that our primary objective is to reach the highest degree of the celestial kingdom. But it seems to me that if we really want that blessing, we ought to be very familiar with the commandments of the gospel; we ought to understand what the road map is; we ought to know it so well that we can be led by the Lord's Spirit so that we will be able to continue toward the celestial kingdom.

As we do so, we will realize when we are drifting in the wrong direction. We will sense when gospel light is being forced out by the darkness of the evil one. Sin, of course, is the best means the devil has of placing a blanket of darkness over us, and when we are doing anything that is unworthy of the celestial kingdom, we do not feel as comfortable and as warm inside as we should. Have you noticed that? I do not suppose any of us has walked this far through life without making some mistakes. And I do not suppose any of us are finished with making mistakes as we sojourn through life. But when we do make mistakes, let us have the good judgment and sensitivity to realize that the Lord loves us so much and wants us back in His sacred presence so much that He has provided us with the great blessing of repentance. He has provided the way for us to correct and adjust our course and to get back on the right path, one that will enable us to return and dwell with Him.

TARNISHED GOLD

I recently read a news account about a man who discovered an old picture in his father's attic. It wasn't a priceless work of art. It was just an old photograph that wouldn't mean much to anyone outside his family, but it was meaningful to the man. He wanted to hang it in his home. Unfortunately, the picture was surrounded by a dingy metal frame that had become crusted over through time and disuse. He decided to remove the frame and mount the photograph in something more acceptable before he put it on display in his house.

As he worked to pry the picture free, he scraped some of the grit and grime from the frame. In the light the exposed metal shimmered with a golden hue. The startled man carefully scraped more of the ugly outer shell away to reveal more brilliant golden metal underneath. Now much more interested in the frame, he took it to antiques professionals, who were able to remove the extraneous material and fully restore a stunningly beautiful—and incredibly valuable—gold-leafed picture frame.

It is interesting to note that the frame had always been golden. Though its owners had allowed the frame's real worth to be covered and obscured, its innate value was not changed. No matter what it looked like, no matter how it was perceived, no matter how it was used, it was still a gold-leafed picture frame. It wasn't until someone was able to peek below the encrusted surface that its real worth was once again understood and appreciated.

The same is unfortunately true for many of us. For one reason or another, we have allowed time and circumstance to cloud our view of who and what we really are. We focus so much attention on the grit and grime of our daily lives that we become oblivious to the solid gold of our souls. Too often we allow the part of us that is golden, the part of us that is eternal, to be covered and obscured by the foibles and limitations of mortality. We forget that we are the sons and daughters of God, that we are good, that we were triumphant in our preexistent state, and that we were sent to earth to overcome our weaknesses, to conquer adversity, to defeat the devil, and to succeed. That is our objective: ultimate, eternal success. No matter what we may think of ourselves, no matter what others may think of us, no matter how ill-prepared and sinful and unsuccessful we may appear to be on the outside, we each have within us the spark of divinity. We are God's children, and that makes us golden.

Of course, the principle of moral agency also extends to us the possibility of failure; but if we fail, it is only because we choose to do so. "Therefore, cheer up your hearts," Nephi reminds us, "and remember that ye are free to act for yourselves—to choose the way of everlasting death or the way of eternal life" (2 Nephi 10:23). Not one of us was born to fail. Each of us was sent to earth with an assignment—an assignment to succeed.

WE WERE GOOD

The ancient prophet Abraham was given in glorious vision a unique perspective of the entire history of this earth and its inhabitants. He saw us—each one of us—and he saw that we were good. He recorded: "Now the Lord had shown unto me, Abraham, the intelligences that were organized before the world was; and among all these there were many of the noble and great ones;

"And God saw these souls that they were good, and he stood in the midst of them, and he said: These I will make my rulers; for he stood among those that were spirits, and he saw that they were good; and he said unto me: Abraham, thou art one of them; thou wast chosen before thou wast born.

"And there stood one among them that was like unto God, and he said unto those who were with him: We will go down, for there is space there, and we will take of these materials, and we will make an earth whereon these may dwell;

"And we will prove them herewith, to see if they will do all things whatsoever the Lord their God shall command them;

"And they who keep their first estate shall be added upon; and they who keep not their first estate shall not have glory in the same kingdom with those who keep their first estate; and they who keep their second estate shall have glory added upon their heads for ever and ever" (Abraham 3:22–26).

This earth life, then, is a test. We are here to "see if [we] will do all things whatsoever the Lord [our] God shall command [us]." Thankfully, this test doesn't require a perfect score. Because of the loving grace and infinite Atonement of the Lord Jesus Christ—He whom Abraham saw who was "like unto

God"—we can be imperfect, and still perfectly successful. Like that picture frame, we can be tarnished, yet golden.

We all make mistakes. That's part of our human experience. Learning to recognize and overcome these mistakes is an important part of our earthly mission. Unfortunately, there are those among us who become preoccupied with their own imperfection. They seem to forget the solid gold of their eternal souls and the purifying power of the Atonement. It's as though they choose to wallow in their imperfections, and in so doing, they deny the work of their divine Creator and the Atonement of the Savior.

REPENTANCE EQUALS CHANGE

When you stop and think about it, it would be the height of spiritual arrogance for any of us to suppose that we have sinned so extraordinarily as to be beyond the reach of Christ's redemption. To do so would be to suggest that His blood is insufficient, that His power is inadequate, that His sacrifice somehow isn't enough. Even in the case of murder and the sin against the Holy Ghost, both of which sins are doctrinally unforgivable (D&C 42:18; 132:27), ultimately only God can judge the circumstances and intent of those involved. The vast majority of us can "sing the song of redeeming love" (Alma 5:26) at the top of our voices, with hearts full of love and gratitude for the blessing and opportunity repentance affords each of us to learn, to grow, to adjust, to change.

Indeed, change is at the very heart of repentance. Although we often think of repentance as the process through which we are forgiven of our sins and misdeeds, we forget that forgiveness isn't something we can earn or do. It is given freely through the loving grace of the Lord Jesus Christ. The repentance process is, rather, a process of change. It is the process Alma talked about when he taught the people of Zarahemla about having "spiritually been born of God," receiving "his image in your countenances," and "experienc[ing] this mighty change in your hearts" (Alma 5:14). It is the process King Benjamin's followers experienced that wrought such "a mighty change" in their hearts that they had "no more disposition to do evil, but to do good continually" (Mosiah 5:2). It is the process that moved King Lamoni and his household to declare unto their people "that their hearts had been changed; that they had no more desire to do evil" (Alma 19:33). It is the process through which we strip away mortality's crusty exterior to reveal the glimmering gold underneath.

Unfortunately, one of the great dangers of sin is its natural antipathy for the process of change. Sin blinds our eyes to eternal views and deafens our ears to the whisperings of the Holy Spirit. Each unrepented sin places additional distance between sinner and Savior and allows Satan better access to the sin-bound soul. With that access he can pound away at spiritually hardened hearts with lies that have proven effective over the centuries. He convinces those who have succumbed to sin that "It doesn't really matter," or that "One more time won't make a difference," or that "God has already given up on you," or that "You're worthless."

A young friend of mine has struggled with some of these lies. Introduced to pornography at an early age, he has battled different manifestations of moral sin throughout his life at various times and in various ways. Sometimes he has been victorious over temptation; other times he has not. Most recently, he became involved in several inappropriate relationships through Internet chat rooms, resulting in his disfellowshipment from the Church and considerable stress on a temple marriage that has already had much with which to contend through the years.

During the course of long and painful discussions with his wife following this most recent indiscretion, it became clear that although my friend had been through the process of repentance several different times, including official ecclesiastical discipline, he had never experienced the "mighty change [of] heart" of which Alma speaks (Alma 5:12). He had been forthright with his Church leaders and had done all that was required of him, but he had not changed. He had not "spiritually been born of God" and received His image in his countenance (Alma 5:14). And so, despite his best efforts and most noble intentions, his problem resurfaced from time to time.

"I thought I had a real testimony," he told me, "but obviously something was lacking."

He had a great understanding of the gospel and of Heavenly Father's plan for our eternal happiness and peace. But he didn't really understand his place in that plan and his eternal value and worth.

"I knew that I was a child of God," he said. "But, to be honest, that thought didn't give me much comfort. I figured that I was one of Heavenly Father's bad children and that all I had succeeded in proving during this life is that I wasn't one of the 'noble and great ones' Abraham saw."

This young man served in significant Church callings. People praised him for his effectiveness as a priesthood leader, but he was unmoved by their praise. He assumed that he had simply fooled them, that if people knew the truth about him and who he really was, they would know he wasn't what he appeared to be.

But it was my friend who had been fooled. Satan had convinced him that he was fighting a losing battle, so when temptations came his way, it was easy to give in. He was, after all, one of God's bad children; therefore, it was understandable if he occasionally did bad things.

Thankfully, his wife is like most of the good women in the Church whom I have known and is smarter and tougher than Satan. Together with their bishop and an effective counselor from LDS Social Services, she is working carefully with her husband to help him see and understand the glowing truth that glistens beneath the unsightly camouflage of sin. It is a truth she has somehow been able to see since she first met him. It is the truth of who he is, who he has always been, and who he is capable of becoming. It is my friend's ultimate reality, his ultimate truth. And it is golden.

SHOUTING FOR JOY

"Where wast thou when I laid the foundations of the earth?" God asked Job. "Declare, if thou hast understanding. Who hath laid the measures thereof, if thou knowest? Or who hath stretched the line upon it? Whereupon are the foundations thereof fastened? Or who laid the corner stone thereof; when the morning stars sang together, and all the sons of God shouted for joy?" (Job 38:4-7).

I testify that we were there, shouting for joy, as God's sons and daughters. All of us. We are good because we are God's spirit children. He created us to be successful. We each have a personal history of success. We know that we kept our first estate and were among "the noble and great ones" to be held in reserve until these remarkable days when the gospel is on the earth in its fulness. Consequently, much is expected of us. We cannot afford to limit ourselves with a lack of understanding of our divine nature and eternal potential. We must move forward in a dynamic way, confident and secure in the knowledge of the gold that glistens within each of us just beneath the surface of mortality.

ANCHORED TO TESTIMONY

A fervent personal testimony of Christ and His Church will help us move in a dynamic, positive direction. Such a testimony often comes in simple ways. From my own experience, I can testify of this. I accepted a call to go to England on a mission when I was nineteen. In May 1948, the *Queen Elizabeth* pulled into

Southampton, and a group of missionaries, not knowing very much, got off the ship and made their way up to London. There we were met by President Selvoy J. Boyer.

After we had met with the president for a little while, I heard him say, "Let's take them to Hyde Park." We knew about street meetings. We had heard about that in the mission home. Never having participated in one and not knowing quite how a street meeting operated, we headed for Hyde Park. There were about fourteen missionaries. Some of them were en route to Europe. Six of us were assigned to the British Isles. I was standing next to President Boyer when he said, "We will only have time to hear from two of them." That gave me a great sense of confidence, recognizing that very likely I would not be one of the two. Then my name was called to be the second to speak from the little fold-up stand there in Hyde Park.

As I moved toward the stand, President Boyer took hold of my arm. I will never forget what he said: "Teach the gospel." That was a new thought. I was a missionary, set apart, but the reality of having to teach the gospel in that kind of a circumstance was somewhat frightening. I quickly got into my mind that I would teach the principle of baptism. I said everything I knew about baptism in about forty-five seconds. My discourse was rather short and not very effective. As I stepped down from the stand, I thought to myself, "You have a lot of work to do. You have a lot of learning to do. You have a lot of preparation to do in order to accomplish the purpose for which your Heavenly Father has sent you to England."

I gained my testimony of the truthfulness of the restored gospel of Jesus Christ during my two years as a missionary. I came to know the reality of the Joseph Smith story, which I read with an entirely different intensity as a missionary than I had ever read it before. I had impressed upon my soul the fact that the Prophet Joseph Smith went into the grove near his home in Palmyra, New York, and there knelt and supplicated our

Heavenly Father, wanting to know which of all the churches was true. The Father and the Son really did appear to him, and the Father spoke to him, saying, "This is My Beloved Son. Hear Him!" (Joseph Smith–History 1:17). That the Savior of the world, our Redeemer, our Lord, our God, our very best friend, spoke to that young prophet on that occasion became a reality to me.

Because of my missionary experience, I became anchored to a testimony of the Savior and to the reality of the restoration of the Church of Jesus Christ through the Prophet Joseph Smith. I stood on other occasions in Hyde Park and on many other street corners in the British Isles and bore my testimony that Joseph Smith is a prophet of God, that the gospel had been restored in its fulness, and that the priesthood and authority to bless mankind is once again upon the earth. The more I bore my testimony, the more it became a part of me.

After I returned home, my testimony gave me the direction and the faith I needed to find the girl of my dreams who would support me in my Church callings and in all my duties and help me live the teachings of the gospel. My understanding of the gospel has given me guidance on the kind of husband, father, and grandfather I should be. My testimony, gained in my youth, has helped me respond to every call in the Church, including my current and overwhelming call to be a member of the Quorum of the Twelve Apostles. My testimony, obtained a long time ago on the street corners of England, has grown line upon line and precept upon precept until I can now stand and testify as a special witness of the Lord Jesus Christ that our Savior lives. He is the Son of God our Eternal Father. My life has never been the same since I anchored my soul to the truths of the restored gospel of Jesus Christ.

Let's return for a moment to the analogy of the ship's anchor, especially the massive anchor chain. Suppose a beautiful sailing ship had been manufactured from the finest materials and had been reinforced and strengthened for the roughest seas. The mast and sails had been prepared carefully and were sturdy and seaworthy. Suppose the anchor was above standard in size and weight and craftsmanship. But suppose that by some inadvertent error, the chain attached to the anchor was inferior and weak. Imagine what would happen the first time the anchor was lowered or the first time a strong wave tried to push the anchored ship out to sea. If any link of the chain holding the anchor broke, the anchor would be left to rust on the bottom of the ocean floor and the ship would drift and perhaps be destroyed.

The comparison to our lives is clear. The links that enable our personal anchor of faith and testimony to keep us safe and secure are the simple doctrines and teachings of the gospel.

THE GOSPEL LINK OF PRAYER

For example, can you see the value of the gospel link of personal prayer? Thanking your Heavenly Father for your blessings will help you remain secure. As you pray, may I encourage you to think of Him to whom you are talking. I have heard missionaries pray, I have heard my own children pray, I have heard others pray, and sometimes I get the feeling that we really do not understand who it is we are addressing. I do not believe any of us would go to a supervisor or even a friend here on earth and report to him as we sometimes have a tendency to report to Heavenly Father. Be prepared in every way to build your communication with your Heavenly Father, to be entitled to the inspiration of the Holy Ghost. Keep this link in your anchor chain strong and vibrant through daily use.

Shortly after I was called to the First Quorum of the Seventy, a solemn assembly was held in eastern Canada for all of the priesthood leaders. The First Presidency, one of the Twelve, and one of the assistants to the Twelve traveled to Canada to participate. It was a glorious experience. As the mission president in

Toronto, I had the responsibility for making many of the arrangements.

At the end of the solemn assembly, we had a light dinner for the Brethren, and then I drove the First Presidency to the hotel where they were staying. I might mention that I have never driven more carefully in all my life than when I had such precious cargo in my car.

When we arrived at the hotel, the Brethren bade me good night and went to the ninth floor. I noticed that President Spencer W. Kimball's secretary, Arthur Haycock, had been detained in the lobby, so I went over and asked him if I could take the key up to President Kimball so that he might get into his room. He appreciated my offering to do that and handed me the key. I took the elevator to the ninth floor and went down the hall. There, standing in the doorway, were President Kimball and President N. Eldon Tanner. As I approached them, I said, "President, here is your key. I thought I'd bring it up to you so you could get in and have a good night's rest."

He thanked me for that in his loving way. Then President Tanner took my arm and said, "Russ, how would you like to come in and have prayer with us?" Of course, I had never had that experience before and gratefully accepted his invitation. I went into President Tanner's room with him and President Kimball. A moment or two later, President Marion G. Romney and the other Brethren came in. I was overwhelmed. I have to tell you that tears welled up in my eyes as we knelt down around that bed.

I was kneeling next to President Tanner when President Kimball said, "Eldon, this is your room. Who would you like to have pray?" I think President Tanner sensed what was happening to me, for he said, "President, we would like you to pray." And then I heard a prophet pray. I would like you to understand that I learned a great lesson in that prayer. I felt the Spirit as I had never felt it before—you can understand it—for when a prophet talks to God, it is close friends speaking. From this special experience, my testimony of the reality of God our Eternal Father and His Beloved Son, the Lord Jesus Christ, was greatly increased, and I knew I had listened to their prophet on earth pray.

In President Kimball's short but humbly sincere prayer, he said this, among other things: "Heavenly Father, we pray above everything else that the labors of this day have been acceptable unto Thee." That penetrated my heart like nothing else ever has on the principle of prayer. Oh, that every one of us might always be found closing the day pleading with the Lord that the efforts of that day had been acceptable unto Him! There is great power in that. There is great strength in understanding that He is our Father, that we are His sons and daughters, and that we are on a journey through mortality that is essential to His plan for our eternal happiness and joy.

Other Links in the Gospel Chain

There are, of course, other links in the gospel chain that will help to keep us safely anchored to our personal testimonies. Can you see another gospel link being the Word of Wisdom? By faithfully living the Lord's law of health, that link in the chain will help us keep our physical bodies strong. At the same time, we "shall find wisdom and great treasures of knowledge, even hidden treasures" (D&C 89:19) that will keep us spiritually strong and help us be more committed to gospel principles.

Another link is the law of tithing. Paying a full tithe is not a matter of money; it is a matter of faith. We can pay a full tithe regardless of our income, if we develop the faith to do so. The Lord surely will "open . . . the windows of heaven" (Malachi 3:10) as He has promised to those who are obedient to this commandment.

How about the links of honesty, moral purity, service to others, attendance at church meetings, and studying the scriptures, to name just a few? These links of the gospel anchor chain may seem somewhat elementary, but they are as important as the anchor of faith and testimony itself. Remember, a chain is only as strong as its weakest link. We must take care every day to examine our own chain to anchor our souls to the gospel of Jesus Christ and keep bright our faith in Him. We must take care that we do not develop any weak links that could make us vulnerable to the influence of the devil.

One good way to keep every link strong is to partake of the sacrament each week. The sacrament is a renewal and a reminder of our covenants with the Lord. What a great time for personal introspection and reflection on our life during the past week. Make the sacrament a time to review your personal gospel chain to see if each link is equal to the task of anchoring you securely to the Church, even as you reaffirm your gratitude to and love for our Savior and Redeemer.

Those who have been endowed in the temple should take the time as often as possible to do ordinance work there. What a strong link that becomes, for it is in the house of the Lord that we can feel the presence of Heavenly Father and His Beloved Son, Jesus Christ.

"A SURE FOUNDATION"

The chain that anchors our souls to the gospel can be as strong as we want to make it through our daily effort. Remember that strengthening our testimony is a lifelong process. Never become discouraged and overwhelmed. Look to the Lord for strength to overcome discouragement and hopelessness. Work on one link at a time and strengthen each until you can feel anchored safely and securely to the gospel of Jesus Christ. Be grateful for the principle of repentance, which provides the way to strengthen any weak links in the chain. If you know that you are anchored to the Lord Jesus Christ, you can find peace and strength in the knowledge that each day you have done the best you can to honor Him.

I am reminded of what Helaman said to his sons, Nephi and Lehi, some thirty years before Christ was born: "And now, my sons, remember, remember that it is upon the rock of our Redeemer, who is Christ, the Son of God, that ye must build your foundation; that when the devil shall send forth his mighty winds, yea, his shafts in the whirlwind, yea, when all his hail and his mighty storm shall beat upon you, it shall have no power over you to drag you down to the gulf of misery and endless wo, because of the rock upon which ye are built, which is a sure foundation, a foundation whereon if men build they cannot fall" (Helaman 5:12).

We cannot fail if we are anchored securely to the restored gospel of Jesus Christ through our faith in Him and if we forge strong links in an anchor chain that will hold us fast to the sure and simple principles of the gospel.

CHAPTER 3

CULTIVATING BALANCE IN LIVING

A link that perhaps we don't think of as often as we should but one that needs to be looked at carefully as we evaluate our progress is that of keeping our lives in balance.

Recently I happened to read again the mythical story of Daedalus and Icarus. You may recall that Daedalus was an architect and sculptor of extraordinary skill who lived in ancient Athens. A series of unfortunate circumstances took him and his beloved son, Icarus, to Crete, where King Minos had Daedalus design a special building that was to be the most extraordinary building in all the world. When the building, called the Labyrinth, was finished, the king was delighted. But he was afraid someone in another land might hear about this unusual building full of crisscrossing passages and want to build something just like it, so he kept Daedalus and Icarus prisoner in its tower.

From this lonely position, father and son could see the blue ocean and watch the gulls and eagles sweep back and forth over the island. Occasionally gulls would land on the tower and peer curiously at the prisoners, as if they wondered why these large, land-bound creatures didn't join them in flight. One day Icarus was throwing stones at the gulls. He killed one of the birds and carried it to his father.

"See how the feathers shine and how long the wings are!" said the boy.

The father took the bird in his hands and turned it over slowly, examining the wings.

"Now, if we had wings," said Icarus, laughing, "we could fly away and be free."

For a long time his father sat silently, holding the dead bird. At last he thought of a plan and said softly to himself, "Then we shall have wings, too."

Daedalus plucked feathers from all the birds that Icarus could catch and began to make two great wings. He fastened the feathers to a framework with melted wax and threads pulled from his linen mantle. When the wings were finished, Daedalus bound them onto himself. He rose into the air, waving his arms up and down, and went soaring far out over the water. Icarus shouted to his father to come back and make another pair of wings so that they might fly away together and leave Crete forever.

When Daedalus had finished another pair of wings, he bound them onto his son. Then he warned Icarus not to fly off alone but to follow him closely.

"If you fly too low, the dampness of the sea will make your feathers heavy and you will sink into the water," said Daedalus. "But if you fly too near the sun, the heat will melt the wax and you will fall."

Icarus promised to be careful, and they took off from the tower and flew away. At first Icarus was obedient and followed closely behind his father. But soon the joy and freedom of flying overcame him, and he forgot all that his father had told him. Stretching his arms upward, he went higher and higher into the heavens.

Daedalus called to him to return, but Icarus could not hear him. The boy's wings bore him higher and higher. As he flew up, the air around him grew warmer. Still he did not remember his father's warning and flew on until he saw feathers floating in the air around him. Suddenly he recalled what his father had told him. He realized that the heat of the sun had melted the wax that held the feathers to the framework. He felt himself sinking, and he fluttered his wings wildly in an effort to fly. He succeeded only in creating such a storm of feathers around him that he could not see. With a wild cry, poor Icarus fell into the blue waters of the sea—known ever since as the Icarian Sea.

Daedalus heard his cry and flew to the spot but could see nothing of Icarus or his wings except a handful of white feathers that floated on the water. Sadly the father went on with his journey, finally reaching the shore of a friendly island. Ever after he mourned his son, and never again did he try to fly (Hamilton, *Mythology*, 139-40).

Just like Icarus, many of us occasionally find ourselves wanting to fly so high and so fast in our various pursuits in life that we may not hear our Heavenly Father calling to us, telling us to be careful that we do not lose our balance. A profession may become so exhilarating, a hobby so enchanting, a project so enthralling, a cause so invigorating, even a Church calling so inspiring that we may want to fly higher and higher within it. Although the pursuit of excellence in any field is a noble and worthwhile endeavor, to do so at the expense of other, equally important aspects of our lives is wasteful and dangerous for ourselves and for our loved ones. We must be very careful to stay focused on things of eternal importance and to make sure that we are controlling our lives—not allowing our lives to control us. For us to do that and to maintain appropriate balance in our lives, it is important for us to think straight at all times.

"LET US THINK STRAIGHT"

Prominently displayed on a wall in my office is a statement that reads, "Above all else, brethren, let us think straight." These were the last words spoken in mortality by my Grandfather Melvin J. Ballard. He had taken a long trip to the eastern part of the United States. When he returned home, after driving from New York to Salt Lake City, he was very sick. He was taken immediately to LDS Hospital, where it was discovered that he had acute leukemia. He never left the hospital.

My father was with Grandfather just before his death. He told me that Grandfather pushed himself up in his bed, looked about the room as though he were addressing a congregation, and said, "And above all else, brethren, let us think straight." Then he died.

I've thought about that statement often throughout my life. What does it mean to "think straight"? As I've pondered the question, it has occurred to me that the Old Testament book of Proverbs has a guide that is helpful: "Hear counsel, and receive instruction, that thou mayest be wise" (Proverbs 19:20). I would suggest that straight thinking begins with careful listening. Those with whom I have associated who are most successful in life are straight thinkers and good listeners; they listen attentively to others and also recognize and listen to the promptings of the Holy Spirit, which is always a companion to the righteous good listener.

The verse in Proverbs suggests that hearing will allow us to "receive instruction" that will help to make us wise—wise enough, hopefully, to think straight. The Lord has spoken quite clearly about the value of such learning.

Through the Prophet Joseph Smith, He instructed His Saints to "receive instruction" and gather knowledge "in theory, in principle, in doctrine, in the law of the gospel, in all things that pertain unto the kingdom of God, that are expedient for you to understand; of things both in heaven and in the earth, and under the earth; things which have been, things which are, things which must shortly come to pass; things which are at home, things which are abroad; the wars and the perplexities of the nations, and the judgments which are on the land; and a knowledge also of countries and of kingdoms—that ye may be prepared in all things when I shall send you again to magnify the calling whereunto I have called you, and the mission with which I have commissioned you" (D&C 88:78-80).

He further instructed us to "teach one another words of wisdom; yea, seek ye out of the best books words of wisdom; seek learning, even by study and also by faith" (D&C 88:118).

He later explained that "the glory of God is intelligence, or, in other words, light and truth" (D&C 93:36) and that "it is impossible for a man to be saved in ignorance" (D&C 131:6). He promised that "whatever principle of intelligence we attain unto in this life, it will rise with us in the resurrection. And if a person gains more knowledge and intelligence in this life through his diligence and obedience than another, he will have so much the advantage in the world to come" (D&C 130:18-19).

Gaining wisdom through knowledge of truth, which the Lord defined in Doctrine and Covenants 93:24 as "knowledge of things as they are, and as they were, and as they are to come," is therefore an essential part of learning to "think straight." We should be hungry for truth, passionate in our search for the facts of life—and eternal life. During the years I was in business, I had a sign on my desk that read, "Don't confuse me with the facts, my mind is already made up." I put the sign there to stimulate my search for the facts and the truth so I would "think straight," insofar as it was possible.

Fact-finding requires time, careful consideration, and—more often than not—patience, as I have learned time and again through the years. A longtime friend of the Church in England was the late Lord Thomson of Fleet. At the age of sixty-seven, Lord Thomson built a great business empire. In a very short time, Thomson Enterprises consisted of 464 different businesses. It became one of the most successful business ventures in the entire world. In his twilight years, he wrote a book in which he explained some of the lessons he had learned through his experiences. He had this to say:

"'Think.' Let us be honest with ourselves and consider how averse we all are to doing just that. Thinking is work. . . . When a difficult decision or problem arises, how easy it is, after looking at it superficially, to give up thinking about it. . . . It is easy to decide that it is insoluble, or that something will turn up to help us. Sloppy and inconclusive thinking becomes a habit. The more one does it the more one is unfit to think a problem through to a proper conclusion.

"If I have any advice to pass on, as a successful man, it is this: if one wants to be successful, one must think; one must think until it hurts. . . . in the early stages, it [thinking] is hard work and one must accept it as such, later one will find that it is not so difficult, the thinking apparatus has become trained. . . .

"I have called this a bank of experience which one builds up in one's early days and draws on heavily when one is older" (*After I Was Sixty*, 106-7).

We can learn to think straight, and when we do we will build up our bank account of knowledge and experience from which to draw in the future. Problems that seem insurmountable to you today will seem relatively simple in the future because you are trained to think straight.

BALANCE IN LIVING

There also needs to be balance in our lives and in our thinking. Brigham Young said: "Some think too much, and should labor more, others labor too much, and should think more, and thus maintain an equilibrium between the mental and physical members of the individual; then you will enjoy health and vigor, will be active, and ready to discern truly, and judge quickly. Is it not your privilege to have discernment to circumscribe all things, no matter what subject comes before you, and to at once know the truth concerning any matter?" (*Journal of Discourses*, 3:248).

Leading a balanced, productive life—maintaining "an equilibrium between the mental and physical members of the individual," as Brother Brigham said—is therefore essential to straight thinking. A friend of mine, the noted author and philosopher Stephen R. Covey, has said: "In my opinion, balanced people read the wholesome literature and magazines which the world produces and they keep up with current affairs and events. They are active socially, having many friends and a few confidants. They are active intellectually, having many interests. They read, watch, observe, and learn. Within the limits of age and health they are active physically, athletically. They have a lot of fun. They enjoy themselves. They have a healthy sense of humor, particularly laughing at themselves and not at others' expense. You can sense they have a healthy regard for and honesty about themselves. They can feel their own worth, which is manifest by their courage and integrity and by the absence of a need to brag, to drop names, to borrow strength from possessions or credentials or titles or past achievements. They are open in their communication, simple, direct, nonmanipulative. They also have a sense of what is appropriate, and they would sooner err on the side of understatement than on the side of exaggeration. . . . [Their] reactions and attitudes are proportionate to the situation—balanced, temperate, moderate, wise" (*Divine Center*, 291-92).

Such balance can be difficult to achieve in a world awash with intemperance, overindulgence, and foolishness. But with straight thinking and a clear focus on that which is most important—not just right now but forever—we can lead balanced, happy, and productive lives, enjoying all of the good and wonderful things that this world has to offer, as well as the blessings of eternity. We can in fact live in the world but not be of the world.

I have a good friend who was the chief executive officer and principal owner of a large corporation. He was known and respected for his business abilities, and his family enjoyed a comfortable lifestyle because of his success. He developed his skills, capabilities, and interests in many areas, and a promising future lay before him. He could have done just about anything with his life, gone just about anywhere, and continued to be more and more successful. Eventually, however, he was called to preside over one of the missions of the Church. When the call came from the Lord, he did not even pause a moment to question. He had been able to maintain balance in his life—that "equilibrium" of which Brigham Young spoke—and accepted the call without hesitation.

But what was to happen to the business? What would become of this great enterprise he had worked so hard to build? He worked things out the best he could, and then he left his business for three years to serve the Lord.

Three years is a long time in the business world, and a lot can happen to a company while the person who has been its guiding light is gone—most of it not good. The company struggled in this man's absence, and some of its assets eventually had to be sold. But toward the end of his mission, a new opportunity arose for my friend. Within days of his release, he was back in business with something bigger, more satisfying, and more financially rewarding than anything he had worked with before his mission.

How did this happen? I suppose he learned from the mistakes he had made with his previous business. He was a better, smarter businessman later in his life. But the most important thing he had learned, I think, was how to think straight and how to manage his priorities, reflecting a healthy balance in his life. He has always been open to new opportunities when they have come along in his church service as well as in his business.

KEEP YOUR EYES ON THE PRIZE

Thinking straight helps us maintain balance in our lives while staying focused on the things that are most important. It helps us to keep things ordered and prioritized even when events swirl around us, seemingly out of control. During the early days of the Civil Rights movement, when so many little battles were being won and lost on individual battlegrounds throughout the United States, Dr. Martin Luther King Jr. used to remind his associates to "keep your eyes on the prize." His point was that although all those little battles needed to be fought, it was important not to get too high with each little victory nor too low with each little loss. "Keep your eyes on the prize." Stay focused on the Big Objective. Make sure you don't lose track of that, no matter what else distracts your attention from time to time.

Do you see how that principle applies to thinking straight? Although there are many things about which we must be concerned in our lives, and many things to which we give time and attention because we choose to, there are certain things that deserve top priority—no matter what else is going on. They constitute "the prize" upon which we must focus our eyes. No matter what else is going on, no matter how many important "little battles" we are fighting elsewhere, we must never lose track of the things that matter most in God's kingdom and what He expects us to do to about them.

President Harold B. Lee gave some very good counsel to us in thinking about the future: "If there should come a problem as to what kind of business a man should be engaged in, whether he should invest in this matter or that, whether he should marry this girl or that one, where he should marry, and how he should marry—when it comes to the prosecuting of the work to which we are assigned, how much more certainly will those decisions be if always we recall that all we do, and all the decisions we make, should be made with that eternal goal in mind: with an eye single to the ultimate glory of man in the celestial world.

"If all our selfish motives, then, and all our personal desires and expediency would be subordinated to a desire to know the will of the Lord, one could have the companionship of heavenly vision. If our problems be too great for human intelligence or too much for human strength, we too, if we are faithful and appeal rightly unto the source of divine power, might have standing by us in our hour of peril or great need an angel of God. One who lives thus worthy of a testimony that God lives and that Jesus is the Christ, and who is willing to reach out to Him in constant inquiry to know if his course is approved, is the one who is living life to its full abundance here and is preparing for the celestial world, which is to live eternally with his Heavenly Father" (*Stand Ye in Holy Places,* 102–3).

You can expect to have divine inspiration and direction to help you in all aspects of your life if you follow President Lee's counsel.

GIVE THE LORD EQUAL TIME

Some time ago, one of my missionaries came to see me in my office at Church headquarters. He had been a fine missionary, and I was pleased to see him. I was also curious about why he had come after so many years. So I asked him, "Elder, how can I help you?"

"President," he said, "I think I'm losing my testimony."

I couldn't believe it. I asked him how that could be possible.

"For the first time, I have read some anti-Mormon literature," he said. "I have some questions, and nobody will answer them for me. I am confused, and I think I am losing my testimony."

I asked him what his questions were, and he told me. They

were the standard anti-Church issues, but I wanted a little time to gather materials so I could provide meaningful answers. So we set up an appointment for him to return in ten days, at which time I told him I would answer every one of his questions. As he started to leave, I stopped him.

"Elder, you've asked me several questions here today," I said. "Now I have one for you."

"Yes, President?"

"How long has it been since you read from the Book of Mormon?" I asked.

His eyes dropped. He looked at the floor for a while. Then he looked at me. "It's been a long time, President," he confessed.

"All right," I said. "You have given me my assignment. It's only fair that I give you yours. I want you to promise me that you will read in the Book of Mormon for at least one hour every day between now and our next appointment." He was hesitant, but he finally agreed that he would do that.

Ten days later he returned to my office, and I was ready. I pulled out my papers to start answering his questions. But he stopped me.

"President," he said, "that isn't going to be necessary." Then he explained: "I know that the Book of Mormon is true. I know Joseph Smith is a prophet of God."

"Well, that's great," I said, "but you're going to get answers to your questions anyway. I worked a long time on this, so you just sit there and listen."

I answered all of those questions and then asked, "Elder, what have you learned from this?"

And he said, "Give the Lord equal time."

What a profound thought. Perhaps we should all engrave that thought on our minds and carry it with us as we walk through this process of mortality. Give the Lord equal time. Give Him His due share of your thoughts, your time, your talent, and your attention. I know that each of us is very busy with all kinds of responsibilities—family, school, work, Church, community, and so forth. There are many demands for our attention, and our time is limited by a wide variety of constraints. As we seek to find balance through managing our time, we need to be sure that we give the Lord His portion. Establish a time and place to study the scriptures daily, even if it's only for a few minutes at a time. Pray regularly. Serve faithfully in whatever capacity a call is extended, including home and visiting teaching, which is the very essence of gospel service. In the great scheme of things, these things take so little time. But the long-term benefits to us and to our families are infinite and eternal, and they will do much to prepare us and our children for the steadily increasing challenges of the future.

That's really what we're talking about here. These are the last days. As has been foretold by God's holy prophets since the world began, they are challenging times; and they are going to become even more challenging. So wherein is our safety? Where is our peace? Where is our joy? Where is our inner security?

My testimony to you is that safety, peace, joy, and security are found only in the life and mission of Jesus Christ, the Son of Almighty God. We embrace His teachings, we give up all of our sins, we repent, we do all that is in our power to come unto Him in a true spirit of discipleship, knowing perfectly well that it is through His grace that we are saved, even after all that we can do. As we give ourselves to Christ, fully and completely, we find safety, peace, joy, and security in Him. That is the ultimate priority that brings balance to our lives. That is the highest accomplishment of straight thinking.

Does that mean we will not have turmoil or personal problems or sickness or family challenges or employment difficulties? Not at all. It simply means that if our faith is anchored securely in our testimonies of Christ, we will be able to cope with whatever adversity comes our way; and we will be able to do so in a positive, faith-promoting manner. Elder Orson F. Whitney reminded us of this important truth:

"No pain that we suffer, no trial that we experience is wasted. It ministers to our education, to the development of such qualities as patience, faith, fortitude and humility. All that we suffer and all that we endure, especially when we endure it patiently, builds up our characters, purifies our hearts, expands our souls, and makes us more tender and charitable, more worthy to be called the children of God . . . and it is through sorrow and suffering, toil and tribulation, that we gain the education that we come here to acquire and which will make us more like our Father and Mother in heaven" (in Kimball, *Faith Precedes the Miracle,* 98).

If we keep the eye of faith focused on Christ, we gain a broader view and an eternal perspective. With that perspective, we can understand adversity from within the context of Heavenly Father's eternal plan for all of His children. We can find balance and comfort in this life in the eternal safety, peace, joy, and security that He promises.

COMMITMENT, NOT CONVENIENCE

Incredible things can happen in the lives of those who have a clear view of the prize and who are able to maintain their equilibrium well enough to think straight. Some time ago when I was in South Africa, the temple president's wife told about a couple from Zimbabwe who had come to the temple just before Christmas.

"During the course of the early evening," she said, "my husband called me into his office and told me that the people from Zimbabwe had no money for accommodation and no place to stay, and he thought we should take them home with us. I did not agree with him and felt that taking care of the people's physical needs when they come to the temple without means to fend for themselves wasn't part of my calling."

The president quietly listened to his wife's perspective. Then he said, "Honey, we are doing the Lord's work, and we live in His home."

"I couldn't argue with that," she said. "Still not feeling too happy about it, I brought them home."

All she could offer the couple to eat was a plate of sandwiches and something to drink. But it was enough. The sandwiches quickly disappeared, as the couple had had very little to eat since leaving their village in Zimbabwe almost sixty hours earlier.

"I felt very ashamed," the temple president's wife said, "and very humbled."

Then the story came out:

"They came to the temple for the first time in 1994 and promised Heavenly Father that they would return at least once a year to renew their covenants with Him. They saved all year for the branch excursion in November, 1995. At the last moment this fell through due to a lack of funds. This was a great disappointment to them. Coming on an excursion was much cheaper than coming on your own. But they had made a promise, and that promise they were going to keep. The whole of 1995, this faithful sister had crocheted articles to sell in South Africa to pay for their stay. So, armed with just their tickets and a case of crocheted articles, they got on the train to keep a promise made fourteen months earlier. Can you imagine how I felt when I discovered that they were quite prepared to sleep at the station at night and try to sell some articles in the morning which would enable them to buy food and then joyfully spend the late afternoon and evening in the temple?

"All they wanted to do was to keep a commitment they had made—no matter what. Sales at the station were slow, so the sisters working at the temple bought whatever was left. They also brought them food to eat on their long trip home. With tears streaming down their cheeks, they told us that they would keep the nonperishables, the biscuits and the sweets, for their children for Christmas.

"Theirs is a story of great faith, sacrifice, and commitment," this good sister concluded. "Mine is a story of gratitude to a wise and loving Heavenly Father who knew that a selfish daughter of His needed a lesson on humility and service. [And may I gently add, thinking straight.] The gospel of Jesus Christ is most definitely a gospel of sacrifice and commitment and not a gospel of convenience."

I had a similar experience in Bolivia. I was standing on the porch of our stake center in La Paz, shaking hands, greeting the brethren as they were arriving for the conference. One brother put out his hand, and as I took hold of it, I noticed that his shirt was a different color from his chest down. He had a great spirit about him, and I asked him his name. Because I had an interpreter there, I also asked him where he came from, where he lived. He told me that he and his companions had been about fourteen hours on the road getting to the conference, walking all the way to the highway. They had to ford two streams up to their chests in water that was dirty, thus coloring his shirt a different color from the chest down. They then had to stand in the back of a truck, he and his three companions, for two-and-one-half hours, coming down from the highlands to the city of La Paz. There he was—dusty, tired, and hungry but ready to receive instruction from the brethren at conference.

"Where are you staying?" I asked.

"I don't know," he said.

"Do you have any money?"

"No," he replied.

We quickly took care of that. I put my arms around him and held him tight, thanking him for his faith and his commitment. Then he taught me a lesson that changed my life forever. He looked at me and said, "Brother Ballard, you are an Apostle of the Lord Jesus Christ. My companions and I would walk for weeks if necessary to come to hear from one of His Apostles what the Lord wants us to do." That is what happens among people who are focused and whose lives are balanced with a clear view of what's really important.

Can you imagine how that made me feel? I was humbled to the core.

UNCOMMON COMMON SENSE

The men and women whom I admire, who are successful in their lives, are generally those who, along with straight thinking and balance, have good judgment and common sense. Lord Chesterfield is quoted as saying, "Common sense (which, in truth, is very uncommon) is the best sense I know of: abide by it, it will counsel you best" (in *New Dictionary of Quotations*, 1084). Benjamin Franklin declared in *Poor Richard's Almanac*, "Where sense is wanting, everything is wanting" (in *New Dictionary of Quotations*, 1084).

Failing to use common sense can be fatal. Consider the pharmacist who was compounding a prescription that called for as much strychnine as you could put on the face of a dime. He didn't have a dime, so he used two nickels. We don't need that kind of common sense. If we will build our bank of knowledge with straight thinking, we will instinctively exercise good judgment and common sense in our most important decisions.

The Lord expects us to follow the counsel He gave Oliver Cowdery: "Behold, you have not understood; you have supposed that I would give it unto you, when you took no thought save it was to ask me. But, behold, I say unto you, that you must study it out in your mind; then you must ask me if it be right, and if it is right I will cause that your bosom shall burn within you; therefore, you shall feel that it is right" (D&C 9:7–8).

Pray for guidance. If you are living righteously, the Holy Ghost will guide your thoughts and you will make good decisions. You are not going to be successful in everything you do.

You will experience some failure and disappointment. Like it or not, that is an important part of the reason we were sent to this world—to experience the vicissitudes of life. I can assure you, however, that your success will be much greater if you learn to think things out carefully and respond to the promptings of the Spirit.

All of which is not to say that there isn't time to enjoy the fun, pleasurable things life has to offer. Men and women everywhere have a desperate need to take time from their demanding routines of everyday life to quietly observe God's miracles taking place all around them. Think of what would happen if all of us took time to appreciate the wonders of nature that surround us and to give thanks to the Creator of this beautiful world.

Some time ago my family and I enjoyed a simple but impressive experience with one of God's creations. I gave my wife, Barbara, a dozen roses for a valentine. They were a delicate peach shade and had a rich scent. Barbara put them in a vase and placed them on the table in our family room. As the days passed, the family watched the blossoms unfold from buds to full flower.

As I watched this miracle, I became curious about roses. I was amazed to learn from a botanist friend that there are thousands of different varieties of roses. Inside each rose is a giant storehouse of genetic coding that develops a seed or a slip into roots, stems, thorns, leaves, colors, and blooms.

Each rose is a compact chemical-processing factory. Using sunlight, the green leaves take carbon dioxide from the air and replace it with oxygen, which we breathe. When other chemicals within the plant react with sunlight, it produces starch that becomes food. As you know, this process is called photosynthesis. Without it the earth's atmosphere would soon be devoid of oxygen, and most living things would disappear from the earth. My friend told me that the chemical energy and the electrical energy our brains were using at that very moment were once sunlight that had been absorbed by the chlorophyll in green vegetation we previously had eaten.

This experience led me to consider the myriad forms of plant and animal life that thrive in astounding balance upon the earth. My esteem for our little roses took on an element of wonder and reverence. I pondered the power of the creative genius who lovingly provided such marvels for His children. I thought then how important it is for every human soul to see and appreciate the glory and grandeur of God in everything about us. Into my mind came the words and message of a beautiful hymn:

> When through the woods and forest glades I wander,
> And hear the birds sing sweetly in the trees,
> When I look down from lofty mountain grandeur
> And hear the brook and feel the gentle breeze,
> Then sings my soul, my Savior God, to thee,
> How great thou art! How great thou art!
>
> *(Hymns,* no. 86)

I felt a deep reverence for both the Creation and the Creator.

In the book of Moses we read, "And behold, all things have their likeness, and all things are created and made to bear record of me, both things which are temporal, and things which are spiritual; things which are in the heavens above, and things which are on the earth, and things which are in the earth, and things which are under the earth, both above and beneath: all things bear record of me" (Moses 6:63).

Truly, the heavens and the earth and all things in them evidence the handiwork of God, their Creator. And in balance they bless our lives.

We need to enjoy life and cherish what it has to offer in order to keep our priorities and thus our lives in balance. Man is that he might have joy (2 Nephi 2:25) in every aspect of life.

"NOTHIN' BUT NET!"

It is also important to savor the fun, happy times with families and friends. We need to appreciate diversions or wholesome entertainments and make sure we don't miss the little events that can add so much to our life experience.

Just after his family moved to a little community in the mountains east of Salt Lake City, a friend of mine became acquainted with a group of young men who were about to complete high school. Several were student body officers. Some held state high school records in athletics. They were outstanding track and football players. None of them had made the high school basketball team that year, however. They became the core of a fairly formidable Church basketball team.

My friend was one of their leaders, and he tried to see their games as often as he could. Toward the end of the season, he arrived early for an important game. He watched as each of the young men came in wearing a letter jacket. Each had numerous awards attached to the letter. Each award signified to the world that the wearer was an achiever. One by one they peeled off these jackets that announced their prowess.

Then Chris walked into the gym. He was a member of the same quorum as the other boys but was several years older. He had, perhaps, little more than half their individual mental capacity. My friend wondered if Chris had come to watch. Then he saw him remove his ordinary, unlettered coat to reveal a uniform.

The game began. The score was close throughout. In fact, with very little time left, my friend's team was ahead by only one point. Then the coach put Chris in the game. Instead of keeping the ball out of Chris's hands so he wouldn't make an embarrassing mistake, everyone was shouting, "Get Chris the ball!" Now, Chris could dribble, but in his own way. He'd run and bounce the ball nearly as high as his head. Someone had taught him to shoot by bringing the ball down around his knees, in a funny way, and throwing it with both hands as high as he could.

His team members got the ball to Chris. He began dribbling to the basket as time was running out. The other team easily could have stolen the ball from him, but instead they opened the way for him to go to the basket. Before he reached the top of the circle, Chris stopped, brought the ball down below his knees and threw it as high as he could. It went nearly straight into the air and came down right through the net. My friend's team went wild. They had just won the game.

Then my friend looked toward the bench of the losing team and saw something that astounded him. They were cheering with the same joyful abandon. He went up to one of those young men after the game and complimented him, but he didn't seem to be listening. All he could say was, "Did you see that? Nothin' but net!"

The written record of that evening would state simply that the Third Ward defeated the Fifth Ward. But I would submit to you that a more complete record would include mention of the straight thinking and balanced living exhibited by young men who understood that there are things in life more important than winning and that personal and group glory can wait long enough to stop and applaud the awkward achievement of one less talented.

The same is true of our pursuit of material things and possessions. I think our Father in Heaven wants us to be comfortable. I think He wants us to be happy. I think He wants us to be secure. Sometimes, though, we may look at those aspects of life perhaps a little more than we ought to. Maybe we ought to be looking at how our resources might be used for the building of the kingdom and the blessing of the lives of others. As we do that more effectively, I promise you in the name of the Lord that your faith will increase, your love of the Lord will increase, your understanding of the kingdom of God will increase.

My mind goes to the Savior's words to His disciples when He said, "Lay not up for yourselves treasures upon earth, where

moth and rust doth corrupt, and where thieves break through
and steal: But lay up for yourselves treasures in heaven, where
neither moth nor rust doth corrupt, and where thieves do not
break through nor steal: For where your treasure is, there will
your heart be also" (Matthew 6:19–21).

OUR UNIQUE PERSPECTIVE FOR ETERNITY

True comfort, peace, and a feeling of eternal security is ours
because we know that we are part of a divine plan designed by
Heavenly Parents who love us. When we understand this truth,
then no one is pressured to compete for worldly position or
acclaim. Rather, we seek spiritual strength and an eternal assurance that we are on the right path. Of course, we want to provide
for our families and do the best we can with the talents God has
given us. But when we consider our unique perspective of eternity, we find that fame and popularity aren't nearly as important
as loving and being loved, status doesn't mean much when compared to service, and acquiring spiritual knowledge is infinitely
more meaningful than acquiring the things of this world.

When our time comes to return to our Heavenly Father to
give Him an accounting of our stewardship while here on the
earth, what do you suppose the Lord will be most interested in?
I believe He will be pleased with all of our honorable accomplishments but will have a special interest in the service—
including sharing the gospel—that we have rendered to others
along the way. Perhaps those experiences where our efforts have
helped others hit "nothin' but net" will be considered by the
Lord our greatest accomplishments.

The eternal perspective the gospel gives us helps bring balanced meaning to our lives and keeps us thinking straight. As
we face the future, our anchor, our testimony of Jesus Christ,
will help us make the right decisions in life, if the gospel links of
our anchor chain remain strong.

CHAPTER 4

LEARNING TO RECOGNIZE
AND RESPOND TO THE SPIRIT

Afew years ago, Sister Ballard and I attended a regional conference in Johannesburg, South Africa. We were impressed with the faith and the special spirit of the Saints. Visiting the African continent brought back memories of my earlier assignments to East and West Africa. I thought once again of the special fast by Church members worldwide in 1985. It provided approximately six million dollars to relieve suffering and hunger, primarily in drought-stricken Ethiopia. Brother Glenn L. Pace and I witnessed firsthand the fruits of generous contributions by Church members when the First Presidency assigned us to go to Africa, assess the needs of the people, and recommend how to make the best use of these special funds.

We visited refugee camps in that arid country. The land was as barren as any I had ever seen. We visited Red Cross centers and field hospitals where the desperately ill were being cared for. Their dreadful, pitiful suffering broke our hearts. We saw sick mothers lying on cots trying to feed and comfort their children, many of whom had the sunken eyes and pencil-thin arms and legs of those in the advanced stages of starvation. This was one of the most heart-wrenching experiences of my life. I had never seen anything that touched my heart so deeply as the anxious yearning for food and nourishment that I saw there.

It occurs to me, however, that even as people in Ethiopia were starving physically because of a lack of food, far too many people in the world today are starving spiritually. Sadly, most of them have no idea where to find real spiritual nourishment. They wander to and fro—pathetic refugees of another kind. Those who yearn for true spiritual light and knowledge can only find it through the power of the Holy Ghost. The Spirit enlightens and gives understanding of the eternal purpose of life. By the Spirit, Church members know the restored gospel of Jesus Christ is true. We should, therefore, feel compelled to share our spiritual knowledge with all of our Father's children by inviting them to pull a chair up to the Lord's table and feast on the words of Christ.

"Come unto the Holy One of Israel," wrote the Book of Mormon prophet Jacob, "and feast upon that which perisheth not, neither can be corrupted, and let your soul delight in fatness" (2 Nephi 9:51). Later, Nephi urged his followers to "feast upon the words of Christ; for behold, the words of Christ will tell you all things what ye should do" (2 Nephi 32:3).

President Gordon B. Hinckley said: "Every member of this church is an individual man or woman, boy or girl. Our great responsibility is to see that each is 'remembered and nourished by the good word of God' (Moroni 6:4), that each has opportunity for growth and expression and training in the work and ways of the Lord. . . . This work is concerned with people, each a son or daughter of God. In describing its achievements we speak in terms of numbers, but all of our efforts must be dedicated to the development of the individual" (*Ensign,* May 1995, 52–53).

For The Church of Jesus Christ of Latter-day Saints to fulfill its divine mission to assist in bringing "to pass the immortality and eternal life of man" (Moses 1:39), all members need to generate an appetite for gospel sustenance. We must "hunger and thirst after righteousness" (Matthew 5:6) before we can be filled.

When I was a mission president, I told my missionaries that I would give anything if I had the power to cause them to thirst and hunger after the things of the Spirit as much as they did for three square meals a day. And anybody who has been a mission president knows that there is not enough food in the world to fill the missionaries. If you don't believe that, may I share part of a letter received not long ago that illustrates my point:

"Our dinner with the missionaries and investigators was scheduled for Wednesday night at 7:00. I started cooking Tuesday evening, continued early Wednesday morning, came home for lunch and continued, then finished Wednesday evening. It was all ready by 7:00. The missionaries came at 7:10—alone. They had looked everywhere for our investigators but were unable to find them. I invited them in, indicating we would eat without them.

"*Eat* is a loose term with a twenty-year-old, hungry missionary. The larger of the two missionaries ate eight bowls of chicken noodle soup with homemade noodles. They finished a basket of crackers with the soup. Next came cabbage salad, with two dinner-plate-size servings for each. The next course was spaghetti with meat sauce. Three large servings and four pieces of garlic bread were followed by another bowl of soup. Dessert was root beer floats which I served in sixteen-ounce cups with two large scoops of ice cream. The meal was completed by two large servings of fruit—watermelon and pineapple. After the meal, the elders assured me that the best part was that I knew how to cook healthy."

And the amazing thing is that missionaries are hungry again just a few hours later. As a people we like to pull our chair up to the table for breakfast and there eat Cheerios or whatever. Then we enjoy lunch, and we feed our physical being again at dinnertime. Somehow we must begin to worry as much—if not more—about feeding our spirit as we do about catering to the demands of the physical body when it is hungry.

Possessing an individual, personal testimony of gospel truth, particularly the divine life and ministry of the Lord Jesus Christ, is essential to our eternal life. "And this is life eternal," said the Savior, "that they might know thee the only true God, and Jesus Christ, whom thou hast sent" (John 17:3). In other words, life eternal—or eternal life in the presence of God and Christ—is predicated upon our own individual, personal knowledge of our Father in Heaven and His Holy Son. Simply knowing about them is not enough. We must have personal, spiritual experiences to anchor us. These come through seeking them in the same intense, single-minded way that a hungry person seeks food.

President Hinckley said further: "The gaining of a strong and secure testimony is the privilege and opportunity of every individual member of the Church. The Master said, 'If any man will do his will, he shall know of the doctrine, whether it be of God, or whether I speak of myself' (John 7:17).

"Service in behalf of others, study, and prayer lead to faith in this work and then to knowledge of its truth. This has always been a personal pursuit, as it must always be in the future" (*Ensign,* May 1995, 53).

We need to cultivate spiritual strength within ourselves before we can ever hope to engender it in others. We must fortify ourselves before we can offer spiritual nourishment to others. President Joseph F. Smith taught us that "it is the right of individuals to be inspired and to receive manifestations of the Holy Spirit for their personal guidance to strengthen their faith, and to encourage them in works of righteousness, in being faithful and observing and keeping the commandments which God has given unto them; it is the privilege of every man and woman to receive revelation to this end" (*Gospel Doctrine,* 41-42).

Experience has taught me that the things of the Spirit come only when they are diligently sought. Testimony—real testimony that will see us through the hard moments of life—comes only to those who are willing to pay the price. Following are some ways we can forge another strong link in our anchor chain, the link of recognizing and listening to the voice of the Spirit.

BUILD SPIRITUALITY THROUGH FASTING AND PRAYER

First, open your heart and mind in meaningful fasting and prayer. When the sons of Mosiah were reunited with Alma the Younger, they rejoiced in their reunion and acknowledged that because they had "given themselves to much prayer, and fasting" they had been given the spirit of prophecy and revelation, so that when "they taught, they taught with power and authority of God" (Alma 17:3). I hope we never let our prayers become automatic. I remind you that the most important part of prayer is not what we say but how well we listen.

When I meet with stake presidents and other leaders at stake conferences, I often ask them these questions: "What does the Lord want you to improve, and what do you want this stake to accomplish this year?" and "What are the major things that must be done, as the Lord has manifest it to you?"

Those questions bring some interesting responses. If I get a blank stare, I counsel with the stake president and other leaders, saying, "Have you taken the opportunity, President, to go out and sit under a tree with your scriptures and read them and pray and ponder and listen for what the Lord might teach you about what He would like to have accomplished in your stake?" Stake presidents have written to tell me they have had sacred, beautiful experiences as they have sat quietly, pondering, praying, and listening.

Fasting and prayer can bring those experiences to all of us. Do not be in a hurry. Allow a little quiet time after you've prayed to the Lord and thanked Him for the blessings of the day. Take time to listen with your heart. Revelation will come to you just as it comes to me through the whisperings of the Spirit. The Lord will place thoughts in your mind and make known to you by the power of the Spirit what you should concentrate on. You must be sensitively attuned to the Spirit to know when the Lord has spoken.

BUILD SPIRITUALITY THROUGH SCRIPTURE STUDY

Second, build spirituality by becoming well acquainted with the scriptures. I am amazed at the number of Church members who do not read the scriptures daily. During my visits at the Missionary Training Center, I often ask the missionaries to respond to this question by raising their hands: "How many of you have read the Book of Mormon from cover to cover and have pondered and prayed about it and know it is true?" Often the hands of fewer than half the missionaries go up. Spirituality comes through paying the price—the price to understand the gospel of Jesus Christ.

I have heard many well-intentioned Church leaders and teachers instruct congregations to find time for daily scripture study, "even if it's only one or two verses per day." Though I understand the point they are trying to teach and applaud the sincerity of that conviction, may I gently suggest that if we are too busy to spend at least a few minutes every day in the scriptures, then we are probably Too Busy and should find a way to eliminate or modify whatever activities are making that simple task impossible. We need to immerse ourselves in the scriptures. The word of God will "tell you all things what ye should do" (2 Nephi 2:3).

Feeding and building our spirits by staying familiar with the standard works of the Church should be a high priority in all of our lives. Spirituality so carefully constructed and well anchored will see us through difficult times. Remember the promise of the Lord: "But the Comforter, which is the Holy Ghost, whom the

Father will send in my name, he shall teach you all things, and bring all things to your remembrance, whatsoever I have said unto you" (John 14:26). The inspired words of the scriptures can be brought to our remembrance in teaching and testifying of the restored gospel of Jesus Christ.

I don't believe we can overemphasize this point. I do not think we can learn anything else in this world that will benefit us more than what we can learn in the standard works of the Church of Jesus Christ. Spiritual knowledge is eternal. It will "rise with us in the resurrection. And if a person gains more knowledge and intelligence in this life through his diligence and obedience than another, he will have so much the advantage in the world to come" (D&C 130:18-19).

Gain that advantage. Pay the price. The scriptures are a conduit for personal revelation. I urge you to intensify your study of them. I promise that your ability to hear the voice of the Lord as communicated through the Holy Ghost will increase and improve.

BUILD SPIRITUALITY THROUGH SERVICE

Third, take an active part in building the kingdom of God through service. Once we have nourished ourselves with the good word of Christ and feasted at His table so that our testimony is strong and vibrant, we are obligated to join with the missionaries in a balanced effort to invite others—beginning with our families—to the spiritual banquet. As the Lord said to His beloved Apostle Peter, "When thou art converted, strengthen thy brethren" (Luke 22:32).

Feeding the Lord's sheep requires each of us to awaken our interest in others. The duty to invite others to partake of the gospel feast does not rest only on the shoulders of our missionaries. That sober and significant duty belongs to each member of the Church, for "it becometh every man who hath been warned to warn his neighbor" (D&C 88:81).

Today, our prophet is calling for enthusiastic and dynamic love for our Heavenly Father's children. He asks us to see the spiritual hunger around us and to respond by willingly sharing our abundance. No power on earth can accomplish as much as one righteous man or woman or boy or girl. And if you think you're just too busy for that kind of dedication of your time and talents, or if you're waiting to devote yourself to God's service more completely "later," may I suggest that you review this with the Lord in prayer and be willing to listen to His counsel. Don't allow yourself to be so busy with temporal experiences that you lose the opportunity for spiritual experiences.

Many years ago, I was called to be a bishop's counselor in a ward of about three hundred members. The bishop organized the Relief Society. The first counselor then organized all of his assigned organizations. I soon learned that I had to staff my organizations with the people who were left after they were finished—and there were not many active Church members left. We needed a Scoutmaster, and I was in charge of Scouting. I searched through the ward roster several times. Where is the Scoutmaster? Where is the Scoutmaster? I couldn't find one. As I looked at the ward list in the spirit of fasting and prayer, a name came to mind. I went to our bishopric meeting and said, "Bishop, you've taken all of the active people. We don't have anybody else. We have only one man who can be Scoutmaster." And I shared with him the name that had been impressed upon my mind.

"Well," said the bishop, "you can't call him. He is inactive. He hasn't been coming to church."

"You have put me in charge of Scouting, and I don't know anything about it," I said. "You want me to organize an effective Scout troop. To do this I am impressed that we must have this man. He knows how to do it; I don't. He is an Eagle Scout; I am a Tenderfoot. Bishop, let's call him to be the Scoutmaster."

The bishop said, "Well, he would have to become active."

"That's your job," I said. "You are the bishop. You have that authority. I'm just trying to run a Scouting program."

I had great faith in the bishop, so together we went to visit this good man. "We have come to visit with you," the bishop said, "and Brother Ballard has something he would like to ask you." With that, the bishop stepped back and pushed me forward.

Through the power of the Spirit, the Lord does work miracles. I looked this good brother in the eye and said, "I've been put in charge of the MIA. Part of the MIA is Scouting. We need you to be the Scoutmaster. Will you come to Church? Will you become active? We need you in this calling."

He, of course, was flabbergasted and said to us, "Well, I'll have to think that over. This is awfully sudden. I am not prepared for this at all." I went back to see him a few days later. He said, "I don't think I can do it."

I said, "We have sixteen boys who need to know about Scouting. Please be our Scoutmaster."

He responded: "Do you think I could really do it?"

"I know you can," I said.

The next Tuesday he came in his Scout uniform with the sash and all the badges. He organized the boys into patrols. He knew the right names for everything. He could even tie the knots. We were off and running with a great Scout troop.

A few weeks later, he called and asked to see me. I went to his home.

"I have to be released," he said. "I didn't keep my promise. I went out and played golf with my brothers, and I slipped up on my promise to keep the Word of Wisdom. I am not worthy to be the Scoutmaster. You will have to release me."

I looked him in the eye and said, "You can't give up. You can't quit. You can't destroy the confidence of those boys. You can't let your wife down. You can't let yourself down. You can't let the bishop down. You can't let me down. You made a mistake; just do not do it again. Next time you go to play golf and think you are going to be tempted, call me and I'll go with you."

That was enough to get him moving forward again to become a great Scoutmaster.

Some years ago I came home from a stake conference and had a message to call him. He was a member of his stake high council and was in charge of Scouting for the entire stake. He asked me to speak at an Eagle Scout banquet. I said I would be delighted. That night they honored more than thirty boys who had earned their Eagle awards under his direction.

About six months later, our old ward was reorganized, and guess who was called to serve as the new bishop? That's right, our Scoutmaster.

The Holy Ghost changed this brother's life. It was the power of the Spirit of the Lord Jesus Christ that inspired us to call him forth out of inactivity to activity. As he served, the Spirit was able to touch his mind and heart to teach him and inspire him to a full life of service.

That same edifying and reclaiming Spirit is available to all of us as we render service in this Church. We don't have to be Scoutmasters or bishops or Relief Society presidents to have the power of the Spirit. In fact, our service doesn't even have to come in a formal Church calling. It might come as a prompting to visit your grandmother even for just a few minutes to tell her you love her and are thinking about her. It might be taking a moment to put your arms around your dad and tell him that you really care and that you think he is great. It might come in counseling a younger brother who has decided at age seventeen that football and girls are more important than a mission. Maybe someone in your family is caught up with drugs or alcohol. The Spirit can help us to know what to do to help them break away from these influences. We need to harness that power in our own lives and in the lives of others as we serve them.

"Me and the Lord"

It is my witness and testimony that the Lord is not very far away. If we learn to recognize the voice of the Spirit and train ourselves to respond to its promptings when they come, remarkable things can happen.

While serving as a mission president, I had the privilege of participating in three stake reorganizations. In each case, a member of the Quorum of the Twelve had the assignment to reorganize the stake presidency and invited me to be at his side when he reached the moment to choose the new president. I had great confidence and peace because I knew an Apostle of the Lord would have the Spirit and would know the man the Lord had chosen.

These were wonderful experiences. We would go to a stake, in which we usually didn't know anyone. Yet, by the end of the day, the Apostle would know who the new stake president should be. He wouldn't hear voices. Angels didn't appear. He simply knew by the prompting of the Spirit, which is the way this work is accomplished.

Shortly after being called as a General Authority, I was flying toward Florida at about thirty-two thousand feet and five hundred miles per hour when it hit me: I was going alone this time—just me and the Lord. I thought to myself: "You better not pick a stake president just because you are impressed with him. You better pick the man the Lord has already called." The Prophet Joseph Smith declared, "I believe that every person who is called to do an important work in the kingdom of God, was called to that work and foreordained to that work before the world was" (*History of the Church*, 6:364).

I believe stake presidents are among those who were prepared before they were born; I believe they were chosen by the Lord before they came to this world.

When we are sent to call a new stake presidency, whether in a stake reorganization or in the organization of a new stake, we generally interview twenty-five to forty worthy priesthood holders, all the while searching for the Spirit to make known God's will. On this day I proceeded with the interviews and had interviewed everybody except two men. So far I hadn't felt what I knew I must feel. I was pleading in my heart, "Heavenly Father, don't let me down. Let me know whom Thou hast chosen to preside over this stake."

Then a man walked through the office door in the stake center. I walked over, put out my hand, and greeted him in unusual terms: "How do I know you?"

"Well, Brother Ballard," he said, "I have met you only one time."

"Where was that?"

"At a youth conference three years ago," he said. "I shook your hand."

"Did you sit with me there?"

"No," he said. "I simply shook your hand as I went through the reception line." And yet he was as familiar to me as though he were my own brother. We called him to be the president of the stake.

This new stake president stood at the pulpit in the Sunday morning session and told this story: "After I was called at about 12:30 P.M. yesterday to be the stake president, Elder Ballard gave me permission to call my mother and father and tell them. I wasn't able to do it until about 6 P.M. My mother answered the telephone. I said, 'Hello, Mom.'

"She said, 'Son, you don't need to tell me. I already know.'

"'You already know what, Mom?'

"'You've been called to be the stake president.'

"'How did you know that, Mom? Who told you?'

"'I was standing at the sink,' she said. 'At about 12:30 an impression came upon me that my son had just been called to be the stake president.'

"My father came on the phone. 'Congratulations, Son! As I

was walking back from the store about 12:30, a voice came into my mind that you had been called to be the stake president.'"

Can you imagine how I was feeling at this point? When I returned home, I told Elder Howard W. Hunter, then a member of the Quorum of the Twelve Apostles, of this experience. "Isn't it interesting?" he said. "The Lord expects us to keep our confidences completely, and yet He doesn't keep His very well. He oftentimes tells people what is going to happen before we even get there, but He puts us through the process. By the power of the Spirit, His will is manifest."

RESPOND TO SPIRITUAL PROMPTINGS

I was sitting at my desk in the Church Office Building several years ago when I felt a prompting to go to LDS Hospital. I had heard indirectly that a dear former neighbor and ward member had been taken to the hospital with a heart problem. I told my secretary to please cancel everything for the next hour because I had to go to the hospital. She reminded me that I had a full schedule. I told her that I knew it would be difficult for her to adjust the schedule, but I knew I had to go to the hospital. I did not know why; all I knew was I had a prompting to go.

I had no idea of the impact of that visit, until I reviewed a letter he wrote to me years later: "When you came to my bedside in the intensive care unit I watched you and heard you administer to me from another vantage point. I saw you with your hands on my head, and I heard you bless me with total recovery, which greatly relieved me. As I opened my eyes I saw a nurse standing over me. I asked if anyone else was in the room. She said that you had been there to administer to me while I was sleeping. All of a sudden my vital signs changed. The doctor decided to wait and see; I was improving so much. In five days I was out of intensive care with no unusual therapy. I had a remarkable recovery in a month.

"I insisted on knowing what happened. My doctor

explained that all of us have a right and a left coronary artery. My right coronary artery was totally obstructed at the heart and still is; the right ventricle is one-half gone. For some reason the blood supply from my left coronary artery spread to all areas of my heart. I have total recovery after eight years. I work eight to ten hours a day, play golf, walk each day, even water ski with care."

Now, I ask you: What would have happened had I not gone to the hospital? The Lord probably would have nudged somebody more faithful and more attentive to duty than I was. But I have come to know the voice, and when I hear it, I move! The way I see it, when my ministry is all over, it will not be any talk that I gave that will be very important in the sight of the Lord; what will be important to Him will be my recognition of His voice and response to His promptings. I constantly pray that the Spirit might direct me to be an instrument in the hands of the Lord to do His will and His bidding.

"You Must Not Go"

Such experiences occur throughout the lifetime of one who is in tune with the Spirit of the Lord. Let me share another experience from the same friend who had the coronary. He wrote:

"You came to my home one very cold, wintry Sunday evening about 9:30 P.M. The wind was blowing; there was deep snow when I opened the door. I guess I was so startled that you had to ask me if you could come in. You told my wife and me that you had just returned from a stake conference in the Southeast; the stake I do not recall.

"You said you were tired but that all the way home from Georgia my wife and I were on your mind, and you needed to talk to us. We were going to the Orient to pick up our son when he was released from his mission, and then we'd board a ship for a cruise up the Yangtze River in China. You sat down and said to us, 'I do not have any idea or reason why you should not go on this trip, but you must not go.'

"My wife literally had a fit, and you gave her a blessing to quiet her down. You were far more popular when you came into the house than when you left. My wife was still going to go pick up our son. We prayed after you left because, unknown to you, there was a payment of eight thousand dollars to be made on the trip the very next day. We decided to believe in the prompting of the Spirit. So the next morning we canceled the cruise. The tour people stated that this cruise had been sold out for months; it was extremely popular; there was no problem.

"The tour people called a few days later and told us that when the ship came into port in Hong Kong it was taken over by the International Maritime Authorities for nonpayment of debt, and it was to be sold to satisfy the judgment. The people who were on the cruise were now stranded in Hong Kong, could get no money, and had no place to stay or to go. I was still recovering from the heart attack, and this would have been a disastrous amount of stress for me. My wife and I then understood again the love the Lord has for our family."

LIVE CLOSE TO THE SPIRIT

The importance of living close to the Spirit is hard to express in words. But the longer I live, the more I know that the Spirit will direct us, teach us, and whisper to us, telling us what we ought to do as parents, neighbors, friends, and teachers.

I visited a stake in Florida years ago. Even though all of the neighborhoods in this stake were filled with people who weren't members of the Church, the stake was having very few baptisms. So we taught the principle of living close to the Spirit and responding to its promptings, especially in missionary work. I encouraged the members to write down a date in the near future on which they would have someone ready to be taught the gospel. I told them not to worry if they did not have someone already in mind. I did not suggest that they write down a name, but rather that they write down a specific date. The key to their success would be to ask for divine guidance in being directed to those who would accept the gospel. I believe if each one of us would set a definite date at least once each year to have an individual or a family ready to be taught the gospel, we would have wonderful success. I explained to the stake president that this would work only if he got involved.

He didn't do anything for six months. Then he wrote me a letter: "I cannot sleep nights because I keep hearing your voice echoing in my ears: 'It will work if you will set the example.' So I just want you to know our family set a date; and our children joined us in our family prayers and fasting as we prayed for help."

The stake president was an attorney, and soon after his family had fasted and prayed for help, a young couple visited his office seeking a divorce.

"I had the most startling spiritual experience I had had for some time," the stake president wrote. "I looked that young couple in the eye and told them: 'You don't need a divorce. What you need is the gospel of Jesus Christ.

"'Now,' he continued, 'I'll tell you what I'll do. I'm so sure that the gospel of Jesus Christ will help your marriage that if you will follow a few steps that I will recommend to you, if I am not right and you still want to have a divorce, I will take care of your divorce and will not charge you one penny.'

"I couldn't believe what I was saying!"

He made an appointment with the missionaries to come to his home. The husband and wife were taught the discussions. The Spirit of the Lord was there and touched their hearts. They joined the Church. That stake president and his family got so excited about following spiritual promptings in sharing the gospel that they brought into the Church no fewer than three families every year. Eventually, he was called to preside over one of our missions.

My own family had a similar experience just as we were about to come home from our mission in Canada. One day I walked into the mission home and called the family together.

"I need your help," I said.

Three of our five daughters were with us and one of our two sons. One daughter said, "What have you done now, Dad?"

"Well, we've got to find another family to bring into the Church," I said.

"But, Father," they said, "we've talked to everybody who lives around the mission home, and we talked to our friends at school. How in the world are we going to do this?"

"I don't know, but we all know that it is the Lord's Church," I said. "We know that, don't we?"

"Yes."

"We all have faith, don't we?"

"Yes."

"So why don't we start praying about it, and then let's just talk to everybody and let Heavenly Father guide us to one more family before we leave in July." This was in April.

My daughter Stacey, who was in high school, came home during the week and said, "Daddy, we have someone to teach." I asked her to tell me about it. She said, "I was walking down the hall in school today, and one of my school friends came up to me and said, 'Stacey, I've been watching you for more than two years. You're different. I've concluded that what makes you different must be your church, and I would like to know if I could go to your church with you on Sunday.'"

Stacey's friend came to church with us. Later, her sister and her brother also came. Her mother and father were separated and contemplating divorce, but they came to the mission home to learn about the Church and to give approval for their children to be taught. They joined the Church because Stacey was willing to call upon the Lord, listen to the Spirit, and respond.

Another example is that of a letter I received from a lady. The letter was quite startling in content. It said, "Dear Brother Ballard. I hate to tell you this, but you are a false prophet. I did what you told us to do, and we had no success. Therefore, you should not be teaching the people to do this." She really got after me. It was not a gentle letter.

I have learned when I receive a letter like that not to answer it for a couple of days so I can think it through a little better. The thought came to me: "I am not going to answer the letter in writing; I am going to call her on the telephone and talk to her."

So, I tracked her down and got her on the phone. "Hello," I said, "this is Elder Ballard."

She said, "Who?"

I said, "This is Elder Ballard of the Quorum of the Twelve Apostles. I am calling you about your letter." There was dead silence for a moment. I repeated, "I am calling to apologize to you. I am terribly sorry that you have had such an unfortunate experience in attempting to do missionary work by setting a date. I am asking you if you will forgive me."

She said, "Oh, Brother Ballard, you didn't need to call me. I just wanted to bring to your attention that it didn't work."

I asked again, "Will you forgive me?"

She said, "Oh, certainly."

I said, "Would you also be kind enough to answer one question?" She responded that she would if she could.

"Will you tell me who you talked to during the time that you were fasting and praying to find somebody for the missionaries to teach?"

Dead silence!

I asked, "Are you still there?"

"Yes, I am."

I said, "Will you tell me?"

She said, "Well, to be honest with you, we didn't do that."

I responded, "In other words, what you thought I said was all you had to do was pray and fast and then in some miraculous way people were going to be put in your pathway?"

Calling her by name, I inquired, "Would you do me a favor? Would you set another date, only this time will you talk to the people in the grocery store, at the service station, in the beauty parlor? Everywhere you go, will you open your mouth and let the Lord help you be successful with this effort?" She was a good sport and said she would.

Less than a month later I received another letter telling me that the missionaries were teaching in their home a family she had met at the grocery store.

Nephi taught clearly that the Holy Ghost is the "gift of God unto all those who diligently seek him" and that "he that diligently seeketh shall find" (1 Nephi 10:17, 19). The stunning reality is that we control how close we are to the Lord. We determine just how clear and readily available promptings from the Holy Ghost will be. We determine this by our actions, by our attitude, by the choices we make, by the things we watch and wear and listen to and read, and by how consistently and sincerely we invite the Spirit into our lives. These are the things that enable us to maintain powerful, enduring links in our gospel chain.

COME UNTO CHRIST

There is only one way to safely and confidently meet the obstacles and opportunities that are part of life's path. If you want to avoid the snares of Satan, if you need direction when the choices in front of you are puzzling and perplexing, learn to hear the voice of the Lord as communicated through the Holy Ghost. And then, of course, do what He tells you to do.

This is a spiritual work. Through His prophet, God has

promised to replace the spiritual hunger that plagues mankind with untold bounty from His own table. All He asks is that we come unto Christ and then do all we can through our families and with the support of the Church to help all of our Father's children succeed spiritually in this critical journey of mortality.

"Behold," said the Lord, "I stand at the door, and knock: if any man hear my voice, and open the door, I will come in to him, and will sup with him, and he with me" (Revelation 3:20).

CHAPTER 5

LEARNING THE
LESSONS OF THE PAST

Another important way we can keep our gospel links firm and strong is to emulate those who have already completed this life's journey. During the Pioneer Sesquicentennial, in 1997, the attention of the Church was focused on the extraordinary events surrounding the establishment of The Church of Jesus Christ of Latter-day Saints in the Salt Lake Valley and elsewhere in the world. Wards and stakes throughout the Church used the year-long pioneer sesquicentennial celebration as an opportunity to honor the Utah pioneers of 1847 as well as the remarkable efforts of our pioneers in every land who blazed spiritual trails with faith in every one of their footsteps.

It was a year for remembering our past and drawing strength to face and conquer the challenges of today from the exemplary faith and courage of those who faced and conquered the challenges of yesterday. As we honored those great pioneers from many lands, we shared historic accounts that often brought tears to our eyes and feelings of pure gratitude to our hearts. Through music, drama, and stirring reenactments, we were reminded of incredible pioneer journeys, both temporal and spiritual.

Looking back on that wonderful time of meaningful reflection and heartfelt appreciation, it occurs to me that we cannot begin to understand the journeys made by those who laid the foundation of this dispensation until we understand their spiritual underpinnings. Once we make that connection, however, we will begin to see how their journeys parallel our own. There are lessons for us in every footstep they took—lessons of love, courage, commitment, devotion, endurance, and most of all, faith.

The faith of the Utah pioneers of 1847 was grounded in principle. They left their homes, their temple, and in some cases their families in search of a place of refuge where they could worship without fear of persecution. There was little they could carry with them in the way of provisions and material possessions, but each wagon and handcart was heavily laden with faith—faith in God, faith in the restoration of His Church through the Prophet Joseph Smith, and faith that God knew where they were going and that He would see them through.

One of those who traveled the Mormon Trail in 1847 referred to it as the "trail of hope." I love that title: "trail of hope." It speaks of the universal yearning of each person to find a safe haven, a community of Saints where hearts are united and hope prevails.

Those nineteenth-century pioneers to whom we paid special tribute during the sesquicentennial year never set out to be heroes, and yet they accomplished heroic things. That's what makes them Saints. They were a band of believers who tried to do the right thing for the right reasons, ordinary men and women who were called on to perform an extraordinary work. At times, they gave in to discouragement and allowed themselves to murmur and complain. But ultimately their faith in God and the man they sustained as their prophet and leader prevailed, and most of them righted their vision and attitudes along with their wagons. In the process they found joy amid the hardships and trials of the trek.

"NOTHING TO FEAR FROM THE JOURNEY"

Nearly seven years before the pioneer exodus to the mountains of Utah, William Clayton wrote to his fellow Saints in England, urging them to come to Zion, not realizing that Zion would soon be in wagons and handcarts moving west. He wrote: "Although we are . . . distant from each other, I do not forget you. But to the praise of God be it spoken, all I have endured has never hurt or discouraged me but done me good.

"We have sometimes been almost suffocated with heat . . . sometimes almost froze with cold. We have had to sleep on boards, instead of feathers. . . . We have had our clothes wet through with no privilege of drying them or changing them . . . had to sleep . . . out of doors in very severe weather, and many such things which you [have] no idea of . . . [Yet] . . . we have been . . . healthy and cheerful. . . .

"If you will be faithful, *you have nothing to fear from the journey.* The Lord will take care of his saints" (letter of 10 December 1840; italics added).

William Clayton later penned the lyrics to "Come, Come, Ye Saints" during the trek across Iowa. He and a host of others learned even more intimately during the thirteen-hundred-mile exodus to Utah that there is "nothing to fear from the journey," if faith is your constant companion.

Is there a lesson in the pioneer experience for us today? I believe there is. The faith that motivated the pioneers of 1847 as well as pioneers in other lands was a simple faith centered in the basic doctrines of the restored gospel, which they knew to be true. That's all that mattered to them, and I believe that is all that should matter to us. Our faith needs to be focused on the fundamental truths that God lives, that we are His children, and that Jesus Christ is His Only Begotten Son and He is our Savior. We need to know that They restored the Church to the earth in its fulness through the Prophet Joseph Smith. Through the restored gospel of Jesus Christ, we learn that our Father's plan for the happiness of His children is clear and quite simple when studied and accepted with real faith.

Traveling from Nauvoo to the valley of the Great Salt Lake in 1847 is not unlike a young missionary from Idaho traveling to Siberia in late 1993 as one of the first Latter-day Saints to labor in that land. Nearly every day our missionaries arrive in countries where they have little knowledge of the language and where the food, culture, and living conditions are often much different from that which they are accustomed to. And yet they go boldly as modern pioneers, not fearing the journey, walking with faith in every footstep to bring to people everywhere the good news of the restored gospel of Jesus Christ.

Our faith can help us be equally bold and fearless during the course of our respective journeys, whether we are parents working with a troubled child, a single parent trying to raise a worthy family, young people struggling to find a place in a wicked and confusing world, or a single person trying to make the journey through life alone. No matter how difficult the trail, and regardless of how heavy our load, we can take comfort in knowing that others before us have borne life's most grievous trials and tragedies by looking to heaven for peace, comfort, and hopeful assurance. We can know as they knew that God is our Father, that He cares about us individually and collectively, and that as long as we continue to exercise our faith and trust in Him there is nothing to fear in the journey.

FAITH IN OUR FOOTSTEPS

Like the pioneers of 1847 who ventured west along a trail that kept them relatively close to life-sustaining fresh water from rivers, particularly the Platte and the Sweetwater, we need to follow and partake of the living water of Christ to refresh our faith and sustain our efforts as we travel the road through mortality.

Life isn't always easy. At some point in our journey, we may feel much as the pioneers did as they crossed Iowa—up to our knees in mud, forced to bury some of our dreams along the way. We all face rocky ridges, with the wind in our face and winter coming on too soon. Sometimes it seems as if there is no end to the dust that stings our eyes and clouds our vision. Sharp edges of despair and discouragement jut out of the terrain to slow our passage. Always, there is a Devil's Gate, which will swing wide open to lure us in. Those who are wise and faithful will steer a course as far from such temptation as possible, while others—sometimes those who are nearest and dearest to us—succumb to the attraction of ease, comfort, convenience, and rest. Occasionally, we reach the top of one summit in life, as the pioneers did, only to see more mountain peaks ahead, higher and more challenging than the one we have just traversed. Tapping unseen reservoirs of faith and endurance, we, as did our forebears, inch ever forward toward that day when our voices can join with those of all pioneers who have endured in faith, singing: "All is well! All is well!"

And how will we feel then, as we stand shoulder to shoulder with the great pioneers of Church history? How will they feel about us? Will they see faith in our footsteps? I believe they will, particularly as they view our lives and experiences from the expanded perspective of eternity. Although our journeys today are less demanding physically than the trek of our pioneers 150 years ago, they are no less challenging. Certainly it was hard to walk across a continent to establish a new home in a dry western desert. But who can say that was any more difficult than is the task of living faithful, righteous lives in today's confusingly sinful world, where the trail is constantly shifting and where divine markers of right and wrong are being replaced by political expediency and diminishing morality?

The road we travel today is treacherous, and the scriptures tell us it will continue to be so until the very end. But our reward will be the same as that which awaits worthy pioneers of all ages who live faithfully the teachings of the Lord Jesus Christ, make right choices, and give their all to build the kingdom of God on earth.

We are the inheritors of a tremendous heritage. Now it is our privilege and responsibility to be part of the Restoration's continuing drama, and there are great and heroic stories of faith to be written in our day. It will require every bit of our strength, wisdom, and energy to overcome the obstacles that will confront us. But even that will not be enough. We will learn, as did our pioneer ancestors, that it is only in faith—real faith, whole-souled, tested, and tried—that we will find safety and confidence as we walk our own perilous pathways through life.

For example, did you know that the vast majority of the Utah pioneers got their first glimpse of the sagebrush, sego lily, salt-flat desert landscape of the Great Salt Lake Valley on foot? Some arrived barefoot after having suffered extreme hardships in traversing more than thirteen hundred miles of prairie, desert, and mountain wilderness. Before the railroad reached the Utah Territory in 1869, approximately seventy thousand pioneers, 9,600 wagons, and 650 handcarts made the trek from Winter Quarters in present-day Iowa and Nebraska to the Salt Lake Valley (Kimball, *Mormon Pioneer National Historic Trail*, 49, 63, 69). Under the most favorable circumstances, the trek took a little more than three months and required millions of steps by each person who walked from the Mississippi River to the Great Salt Lake Valley. In total, billions of footsteps of faith were taken by our pioneers.

Looking back on the trek from our vantage point more than 150 years later, it's clear that each step was worth the effort. We see the fruits of their labors: an international Church, widely honored and respected, with membership well over eleven million individuals and temples being built throughout the world. We see a beautiful metropolitan city glistening in a valley they once saw as arid, dry, and barren, and generations of descendants who are firm and solid and steadfast and true. They had no such perspective of time. All they could see with their natural eyes was the wilderness stretched out before them—a wilderness they had to cross with tired muscles and aching feet. That they did so by the thousands is a powerful lesson for all who face overwhelming obstacles in their own lives today.

In my twenty-five years as a General Authority, I have seen the worldwide expansion of the Church, and I marvel at the results of the work of our pioneers in every country where they, through their faith and sacrifice, established the Church. I share the feelings of President Heber J. Grant, who said, "I can never think of [the pioneers] but I am full of admiration and gratitude, and utter a prayer to the Lord to help me, as one of the descendants of that noble band, to be loyal, to be true, to be faithful as they were!" (Conference Report, October 1919, 7).

LESSONS OF OUR PIONEERING PAST

Other lessons for our time can be extracted from the noble examples that come from our pioneering past.

A few years ago I spoke in general conference about Jens Neilson, a member of the Willie Handcart Company. Jens, a relatively prosperous Danish farmer, heeded the call to bring his family to Zion. In Iowa he wrote that he had let all of his money go to the Church except enough to buy a handcart and stock it with fifteen pounds of belongings per person. The people for whom Jens was responsible were himself; his wife, Elsie; their six-year-old son, Neils; and a nine-year-old girl, Bodil Mortensen, whom Jens had offered to take to Utah. In an early winter blizzard in Wyoming, temperatures plummeted below zero. The

Neilsons had consumed their last pound of flour days before, but somehow they made it over the treacherous Rocky Ridge, urged on by their indomitable courage and unconquerable faith. Tragically, thirteen of the company had died at Rock Creek and were buried in shallow, snow-covered graves—among them Neils, the son of Jens and Elsie, and young Bodil Mortensen.

Jens had arrived at Rock Creek, eleven miles beyond Rocky Ridge, with both feet frozen. Unable to walk another step, he pleaded with Elsie, "Leave me by the trail in the snow to die, and you go ahead and try to keep up with the company and save your life." Elsie, with her unfaltering pioneer courage, replied, "Ride, I can't leave you, I can pull the cart" (Nielson, Journal, in *Wyoming Trails*, 28-29).

Some time after telling that story, I heard about a woman who had listened to my talk. She and her husband were going through a difficult time as he struggled with some spiritual issues, and it appeared that the marriage was going to end. But this sister was touched by the power of that simple story about a pioneer couple who had encountered extraordinary adversity and overcame it by literally pulling together.

"Even when the husband wasn't able to pull any longer, the wife was willing to load him into the cart and carry him as well as his share of the burden," the woman told her bishop. "Maybe that's sort of what I need to do for a time while my husband works through his problems."

That is precisely what she did, and the marriage has not only survived but thrived as a result of her willingness to "pull the cart" while her husband recovered from spiritual injury.

PIONEERING PROPHETS

The pioneer pattern of "faith in every footstep" was also exemplified by those who became the next four Presidents of the Church after the martyrdom of the Prophet Joseph Smith and his faithful brother Hyrum. Brigham Young, upon whom the Lord placed the responsibility to lead the great exodus west, learned early to follow the Lord and to follow the Prophet. Within five months after Brigham and his wife, Miriam, were baptized in the millpond by their home in Mendon, New York, Miriam died of tuberculosis. Responding to Joseph's request to come to Kirtland, Brigham and his small family, with footsteps of faith, journeyed there. In Brigham's words, "When we arrived in Kirtland, if any man that ever did gather with the Saints was any poorer than I was—it was because he had nothing. . . . I had two children to take care of—that was all. I was a widower. 'Brother Brigham, had you any shoes?' No; not a shoe to my foot, except a pair of borrowed boots. I had no winter clothing, except a homemade coat that I had had three or four years. 'Any pantaloons?' No. 'What did you do? Did you go without?' No; I borrowed a pair to wear till I could get another pair. I had traveled and preached and given away every dollar of my property . . . until I had nothing left to gather with; but Joseph said: 'come up'; and I went up the best I could" (*Journal of Discourses*, 11:295).

John Taylor, the third President of the Church, began his journey in Toronto, Canada. Foreshadowing the sacrifices he and his family would make because of their faith, he stated even before his baptism: "If I find [this] religion true, I shall accept it, no matter what the consequences may be." Being obedient, he gathered to Kirtland during the bitter apostasy of 1837. When apostates criticized Joseph Smith, Brother Taylor undauntedly proclaimed, "It is not the man that I am following but the Lord" (in Roberts, *Life of John Taylor*, 37–38, 40).

Wilford Woodruff entered the icy waters of baptism in Richland, Oswego County, New York, on 31 December 1833. He was twenty-six years old and single. He described the circumstances of his baptism as follows: "The snow was about three feet deep, the day was cold, and the water was mixed with ice and snow, yet I did not feel the cold" (in Cowley, *Wilford*

Woodruff, 35). Perhaps in preparation for his journey to the Salt Lake Valley, Wilford's footsteps of faith carried him four hundred miles to Kirtland, where he joined Zion's Camp for an additional thousand-mile trek. As he explained, "Parley P. Pratt told me it was my duty to lay aside all my temporal matters, go to Kirtland, and join Zion's Camp. I obeyed his counsel" (Conference Report, April 1898, 57).

Phoebe Carter was similarly led 750 miles from Scarboro, Maine, to Kirtland, Ohio, where she met and married Wilford Woodruff. Phoebe was barely twenty-eight years old when she determined to gather with the Saints, even though she had to make her trek alone. As she later reported, "My friends marveled at my course, as did I, but something within impelled me on. My mother's grief at my leaving home was almost more than I could bear; and had it not been for the spirit within I should have faltered at the last. My mother told me she would rather see me buried than going thus alone out into the heartless world. 'Phoebe,' she said, . . . 'will you come back to me if you find Mormonism false?' I answered, 'yes, Mother; I will, thrice.' . . . When the time came for my departure I dared not trust myself to say farewell; so I wrote my good-byes to each, and leaving them on my table, ran down stairs and jumped into the carriage. Thus I left the beloved home of my childhood to link my life with the saints of God" (in Tullidge, *Women of Mormondom*, 412).

At that point Phoebe had no idea that her footsteps of faith would lead her on a journey much longer than the 750 miles to Kirtland. They would join with Wilford's in going 1,300 miles through Missouri to Nauvoo and then another 1,400 miles to the Salt Lake Valley.

Lorenzo Snow was born in Mantua, Ohio, near Kirtland. Upon his conversion at age twenty-two, he said: "I made up my mind that I would do my duty and that this principle would be my guide through life. I made up my mind solidly that whatever

I was asked to do in the Church and Kingdom of God, I would try to do it" (Snow, "How Lorenzo Snow Found God," 105).

Faith to Follow

It was not just those who would become leaders who were led by their faith to follow the Prophet. Oliver Huntington's parents left affluent circumstances that included a 230-acre farm with a good stone house and two frame barns and with their family took their journey to join with the Saints. After they left all behind, Oliver wrote, "It was a torment to each, to see the other in want and still more see their children cry for bread and have none to give them nor know where the next was coming from." On their journey by river boat, all of their goods were lost. He recorded, "We never saw any thing more of our goods, which left us as bare as a sheared sheep." He certified the faith of this family, saying he never heard his parents "utter a murmuring or complaining word against any of the authorities of the church, or express a doubt of the truth of the work" (Diary, 28–29).

John Tanner, of Lake George, New York, loaded all his earthly goods into his wagon because the Lord told him in a dream to go to Kirtland. He was perhaps the wealthiest man in the Church at that time and laid out tens of thousands of dollars to see the temple completed. All he had left for the thousand-mile trip from Kirtland to Missouri was a cart, a borrowed wagon, one horse of his own and three that were borrowed, twenty dollars, and a keg of powder. He took his family, eleven persons in all. They ran out of food on the way and had to beg for buttermilk and sometimes other food to stay alive. A young daughter died during this trip. Was he bitter? No! Faithful through all he endured, his simple response to those who were critical was simply, "Well, if others have come up easier, they have not learned so much" ("Sketch of an Elder's Life," in *Scraps of Biography,* 15).

Emily Partridge, the daughter of the first bishop of the

Church in this dispensation, remembered leaving their comfortable home in Painesville, Ohio, when she was just eight years old. She described how they found an "old log cabin that had been used for a stable. . . . There was one large room, and a lean to, but that was not of much use, as the floor was nearly all torn up, and the rats and rattlesnakes were too thick for comfort. There was a large fireplace in the one habitable room, and blankets were hung up a few feet back from the fire and the two families, fifteen or sixteen in number, were gathered inside of those blankets to keep from freezing for the weather was extremely cold, so cold that the ink would freeze in the pen as father sat writing close to the fire." She summarized their experience: "Times were hard and we were very destitute, having been robbed and driven from our homes and possessions so many times, and having had much sickness" ("Autobiography," *Woman's Exponent* 13 [1884]: 138).

Much the same spirit is reflected in a letter from Emma Smith to her prophet husband as the Saints were finally driven to Illinois because of the Extermination Order issued in Missouri. At that time, Joseph and Hyrum and others were still unjustly incarcerated in the cold, dark dungeon that was Liberty Jail. Wrote Emma: "No one but God, knows the reflections of my mind and the feelings of my heart when I left our house and home, and almost all of everything that we possessed excepting our little children, and took my journey out of the state of Missouri, leaving you shut up in that lonesome prison. . . . the reflection is more than human nature ought to bear. The daily sufferings of our brethren . . . and those on the other side of the river would beggar the most lively description" (in Jessee, *Personal Writings of Joseph Smith,* 388–89). During their seventeen years of marriage, Joseph and Emma lived in at least a dozen homes across five states. They trudged more than seventeen hundred miles and buried six of their eleven children.

It was faith that fortified the Prophet Joseph through the

years of persecutions and trials which ultimately led to Carthage Jail. No greater footsteps of faith have been taken in our dispensation than those of Joseph and his elder brother Hyrum as they made their way to Carthage, trusting in the Lord, yet knowing in their hearts that their ministry was coming to a close. I can only imagine the feelings in my great-great-grandfather's heart as he stopped to lift his young son Joseph F. Smith in his arms to bid him farewell.

In paying tribute to these noble souls, President Gordon B. Hinckley has admonished us: "Let us never forget that we have a marvelous heritage received from great and courageous people who endured unimaginable suffering and demonstrated unbelievable courage for the cause they loved. You and I know what we should do. God help us to do it when it needs to be done" (*Ensign*, November 1991, 59).

DIFFERENT MOUNTAINS TO CLIMB

We face different challenges today—different mountains to climb, different rivers to ford, different valleys to make "blossom as the rose" (Isaiah 35:1). But even though the wilderness we've been given to conquer is decidedly different from the rough and rocky trail to Utah and the barren landscape that our pioneer forebears encountered in 1847, it is no less challenging and trying for us than it was for them. And it is certainly no less important for all of us to keep our eyes on the prophet, our shoulders to the wheel, and our feet firmly planted on the trail of faithfulness.

Our struggle is found in living in a world steeped in sin and spiritual indifference, where self-indulgence, dishonesty, and greed seem to be present everywhere. Today's wilderness is one of confusion and conflicting messages. The pioneers had to battle the wilderness of rocky ridges and dusty mountain trails with their faith focused on Zion and the establishment of the Church in the Salt Lake Valley. We too must focus on Zion and put our faith to work in building up the kingdom of God in our homes, wards, and branches. We must have the same kind of faith, the same willingness to give our all, even our lives if necessary, to the great cause of The Church of Jesus Christ of Latter-day Saints. Somehow each one of us needs to commit to the service of the Lord with the same diligence and faith that our forefathers did. We must ever be on our guard that we do not become casual in teaching the gospel to our children in our own homes, paying our tithing, living the Word of Wisdom, abiding by the law of chastity, and being honest and trustworthy in all that we do. We must faithfully do home and visiting teaching and attend the temple and our Sunday meetings. If we become casual in these things, we will lose the sense of urgency to keep the commandments. Lucifer will find a way to dull our commitment and our love for the Lord, and we will become lost in the wilderness of the world.

Real faith, our anchor in the storm, born of the Spirit, affects our actions and our attitudes. When we truly believe, we ask not "What do I have to do?" but rather "What more can I do?" When we truly believe, and when that belief is confirmed upon our souls by the Holy Spirit, faith becomes a causative force in our lives, driving every thought, word, and deed heavenward. That's what it means to walk with "faith in every footstep." It was so for our pioneer ancestors, and it must be so for us today. Our journey today is decidedly different from the one taken 150 years ago. We're not fighting wolves and frostbite; we're fighting pornography conveniently found on the Internet as well as in many other places. We fight drugs and abuse, filth and sleaze of all kinds. We're not struggling to keep our families alive in a world fraught with the cruelties of nature; we're struggling to keep our values alive in a world that mocks our standards and deems it politically incorrect to live them. We're not working to physically push handcarts over steep mountains and through deep snow drifts; we're working to spiritually push ourselves to overcome discouragement and complacency.

Our journey is different, but the trail we must follow is the same. It is the trail of faith, and if we keep our feet firmly planted on that trail, we will be just as successful in facing our challenges and trials in conquering the wilderness of worldly things as our pioneer ancestors were in facing theirs. Just as it required faith for the widowed Mary Fielding Smith to pack up her family and face the trek to the mountains of Utah alone, so it requires faith for us to remain true and faithful today. Just as we marvel at the faith it required for thousands of men, women, and children to willingly endure the untold sacrifices of pioneer life, so someday will they marvel at the faith required of valiant Latter-day Saints today to willingly endure the untold sacrifices of contemporary living in order to remain true and faithful to sacred covenants and commitments.

Remember, through our study of the scriptures, our heartfelt prayers, and our diligent obedience to God's laws, we place our feet in the footsteps of noble pioneers, of faithful Saints through the ages, even from Adam down to our day. We place our feet in the footsteps of prophets and Apostles and even of the Master Himself. As we follow in their footsteps of faith, we find ourselves grasping hold of the iron rod, unhesitatingly following a pathway through the worldly mists of darkness that leads us to faithfulness, to service, to temple worship, and on to the kingdom of God.

Learning from Ancient Pioneers

To this point we have considered only the lessons we can learn from those who set such a powerful example of faith and courage in the early days of this dispensation of the gospel. Our vision need not be limited to those relatively recent pioneers. Throughout history there have been pioneers whose example should be studied and cherished as we look for inspiration in meeting the daily challenges of our lives today. We must never lose sight of the fact that pioneers of the gospel have gone before us, beginning with Father Adam and Mother Eve when they were cast out of the Garden of Eden, a place of beauty where God had made "to grow every tree, naturally, that is pleasant to the sight of man" (Moses 3:9) into a world of thorns and thistles, where "by the sweat of thy face shalt thou eat bread" (Moses 4:25). With faith marking the footsteps of their journey, Adam and Eve, his wife, listened as they were taught the central message of the gospel, that of a Savior to atone for their transgressions. They responded to their changed circumstances by expressing joy for their redemption and, blessing "the name of God, . . . they made all things known unto their sons and their daughters" (Moses 5:12).

Similarly, it was no small thing for Noah to heed the command from God to build an ark of gopher wood before any drops of rain fell. I am sure his friends and neighbors scoffed and laughed as he and his sons worked on the ark and as Noah tried to convince the people to repent of their wickedness so as not to bring destruction upon themselves. What a powerful example of faith and dedication to that which he knew was right—no matter the cost of ridicule and scorn.

It was no small thing for Abraham, with just his wife, his father, and one or two others to follow the Lord's command to "get thee out of thy country, and from thy kindred, and from thy father's house, unto a land that I will show thee" (Abraham 2:3). There was faith in every footstep for Abraham, after receiving the promise that his seed would become as numerous as the sands of the sea, to obediently walk the trail toward the place of sacrifice, again following the Lord's command: "Take now thy son, thine only son Isaac, whom thou lovest, and get thee into the land of Moriah; and offer him there for a burnt offering" (Genesis 22:2). Thankfully, God was only testing him, and his beloved son Isaac was allowed to live. But can we be as faithful and as willing to lay on the altar of our lives all that God requires of us? Another great pioneering lesson for us to learn.

Moses, who had been reared in Pharaoh's court, accepted a call from God to lead his people out of bondage. Only great faith would have enabled him to stand before Pharaoh and declare the plagues that were to come on Egypt until the 430 years of Israelite bondage were brought to an end. It is not possible to count the footsteps of faith he walked during the forty years he led Israel as they wandered in the wilderness before the Lord would permit them to enter the promised land, a land the Lord told Moses he would "give . . . unto thy seed, . . . but thou shalt not go over thither. So Moses the servant of the Lord died there in the land of Moab" (Deuteronomy 34:4–5).

It was no small thing for Lehi, a man living with his family in relative comfort in Jerusalem, to leave behind all his wealth and take his family into the wilderness, not knowing beforehand where they should go, because he had seen a vision that Jerusalem was to be destroyed. It was no small thing for young Nephi to accept his father's prophetic teachings and withstand the tauntings and beatings from older brothers who did not. Faith in every footstep carried him back to Jerusalem to obtain the plates of brass from Laban and then to build a ship on which his family would cross the ocean. It was no small thing for Alma to accept the call to repentance issued by Abinadi and in quiet footsteps of faith to privately teach the words of Abinadi to the people. He and his followers were forced to flee into the wilderness to escape wicked King Noah's attempts to have them killed. And they did "gather themselves together to teach the people, and to worship the Lord their God" (Mosiah 18:25).

It was no small thing for Peter and his brethren to leave their trades and follow the Savior. To the fishermen, the Savior gave the call: "Follow me, and I will make you fishers of men. And they straightway left their nets, and followed him" (Matthew

4:19–20). From those first footsteps of faith, the Twelve walked with the Savior during His mortal ministry, sometimes wavering but always learning and drawing strength from Him. Their journey took them from Calvary to the outpouring of the Spirit at the marvelous day of Pentecost when Peter stood forth boldly proclaiming the resurrection of Christ and calling all to "repent, and be baptized every one of you in the name of Jesus Christ for the remission of sins" (Acts 2:38).

Peter, Philip, Barnabas, and Mark faithfully journeyed through many parts of the world bordering the Mediterranean Sea to establish and strengthen the Church. Likewise, Paul's footsteps of faith took him to Mars Hill and the declaration of who the unknown God really was, to the stirring testimony before King Agrippa, and to suffering shipwreck while a prisoner being transported to Rome. Paul was beaten many times, imprisoned frequently, stoned nearly to death, shipwrecked a total of three times, robbed, and nearly drowned. Starving, freezing, and poorly clothed, yet was Paul faithfully consistent in his service. None of us has been called upon to suffer so much as a consequence of our Church callings, and yet we struggle with the small demands that are made. Oh, that we could all follow Paul's pioneering example and serve as he served in the meridian of time.

Valiant Moroni walked footsteps of faith for many years, footsteps which very few are called upon to tread—alone, without the encouragement and support of others who believe in Christ. In his poignant words: "I had supposed not to have written more, but I have not as yet perished; and I make not myself known to the Lamanites lest they should destroy me. . . . And I, Moroni, will not deny the Christ; wherefore, I wander whithersoever I can for the safety of mine own life" (Moroni 1:1, 3).

THE GREATEST PIONEER OF ALL

Of course, the greatest pioneer of all is the Savior. As we note in song, "He marked the path and led the way, and every point defines" ("How Great the Wisdom and the Love," *Hymns,* no. 195). He declared: "Behold I have given unto you my gospel, and this is the gospel which I have given unto you—that I came into the world to do the will of my Father, because my Father sent me. And my Father sent me that I might be lifted up upon the cross" (3 Nephi 27:13-14). No footsteps in time or eternity have required such perfect faith as did the footsteps of the Savior. And no pioneering example could be more profound for any of us than the example Christ set for us throughout His mortal ministry, and throughout all time and eternity.

We are all bound together—pioneers from the nineteenth, twentieth, and twenty-first centuries and more—in our great journey to follow the Lord Jesus Christ and to allow His atoning sacrifice to work its miracle in our lives. As we appreciate the footsteps of faith walked by Joseph Smith and his followers from Palmyra to Carthage Jail and across the Great Plains, and the paths followed by holy men and women from Adam's time to this, we should ever stand in reverential awe as we contemplate the path trod by the Master. His faithful footsteps to Gethsemane and to Calvary rescued all of us and opened the way for us to return to our heavenly home.

Let us remember that the Savior is the Way, the Truth, and the Life. There can be no greater promise than to know that if we are faithful and true, we will one day be safely encircled in the arms of His love (D&C 6:20). He is always there to give encouragement, to forgive, and to rescue. Therefore, as we exercise faith and are diligent in keeping the commandments, we have nothing to fear from the journey.

A few years ago, I stood with three of my grandsons on the crest of the hill known as the Eminence. Looking down at the Sweetwater where the Willie Company was stranded, cold and starving, we read from their journals of the joy of their rescue. As John Chislett wrote: "Just as the sun was sinking beautifully behind the distant hills . . . several covered wagons . . . were seen coming towards us. The news ran through the camp like wild-fire. . . . Shouts of joy rent the air; strong men wept till tears ran freely down their furrowed and sun-burnt cheeks. . . . That evening, for the first time in quite a period, the songs of Zion were to be heard in the camp. . . . With the cravings of hunger satisfied, and with hearts filled with gratitude to God and our good brethren, we all united in prayer, and then retired to rest" (in Hafen and Hafen, *Handcarts to Zion,* 106–7).

At that moment, standing on the same hill from which the Willie Company first saw their rescuers, I contemplated the joy that will fill our hearts when we fully come to know the eternal significance of the greatest rescue—the rescue of the family of God by the Lord Jesus Christ. For it is through Him that we have promise of eternal life. Our faith in the Lord Jesus Christ is the source of spiritual power that will give you and me the assurance that we have nothing to fear from the journey. I know the Lord Jesus Christ lives and our unwavering faith in Him is the greatest lesson we can learn from the past. It is the anchor that will see us safely along our journey through life.

CHAPTER 6

STANDING FOR TRUTH
AND RIGHTEOUSNESS

No link in our gospel anchor chain should be kept in better working order nor be more polished than our determination to stand for truth and righteousness.

Through the years I've attended a number of groundbreaking ceremonies for various Church buildings all around the world—more than I can even remember, I'm afraid—but for some reason, one stands out in my mind, and I can remember it as vividly as if it were yesterday.

It was the spring of 1956. My family and I gathered with other members of the Holladay 7th Ward on a hillside near Mount Olympus in the Salt Lake Valley. Under the direction of our stake president, G. Carlos Smith, we broke ground for the construction of a new ward building. At the time that ward was created, we had a total of 373 members—more than half of them, as I recall, under the age of twelve. I was serving as second counselor to Bishop William Partridge at the time. Under his inspired leadership, this little band of people began the task of building their new meetinghouse, which at that time meant not only doing as much of the actual work as possible during the

construction process but also raising half the cost of construct-
ing a new building.

Just as we were getting close to the end of the project, the
ward was divided, and I was called to be bishop of the new
Holladay 12th Ward. One of the most important leadership
experiences in my life came several weeks before the announced
dedication of the building. Our ward, composed mostly of
young families like ours who were struggling to make ends
meet, needed to raise the final thirty thousand dollars required
to pay our share of the cost. I fasted and prayed, asking for help
from Heavenly Father to know what to say to our ward members regarding this obligation. We had already pressed them
hard for donations, and they had willingly contributed money
and personal labor beyond anything I had believed possible. But
we still needed to raise the last thirty thousand dollars.

As the brethren gathered for priesthood meeting one
Sunday morning, I felt impressed to read to them the testimony
my Grandfather Ballard bore to the First Presidency and the
Council of the Twelve on 7 January 1919, the day he was
ordained an Apostle. I quote just a small portion of his testimony here:

"I know . . . as I know that I live . . . that this is God's work
and that you are His servants. . . . I remember one testimony,
among the many testimonies which I have received. . . . Two
years ago, about this time, I had been on the Fort Peck
Reservation for several days with the brethren, solving the problems connected with our work among the Lamanites. Many
questions arose that we had to settle. There was no precedent
for us to follow, and we just had to go to the Lord and tell Him
our troubles, and get inspiration and help from Him.

"On this occasion I had sought the Lord, under such circumstances, and that night I received a wonderful manifestation
and impression which has never left me. I was carried to this
place—into this room. I saw myself here with you. I was told

there was another privilege that was to be mine; and I was led into a room where I was informed I was to meet someone. As I entered the room I saw, seated on a raised platform, the most glorious being I have ever conceived of, and was taken forward to be introduced to Him. As I approached He smiled, called my name, and stretched out His hands toward me. If I live to be a million years old I shall never forget that smile. He put His arms around me and kissed me, as He took me into His bosom, and He blessed me until my whole being was thrilled. As He finished I fell at His feet, and there saw the marks of the nails; and as I kissed them, with deep joy swelling through my whole being, I felt that I was in heaven indeed.

"The feeling that came to my heart then was: Oh! If I could live worthy, though it would require four-score years, so that in the end when I have finished I could go into His presence and receive the feeling that I then had in His presence, I would give everything that I am or ever hope to be!" (in Ballard, *Melvin J. Ballard,* 65–66).

The Spirit of the Lord touched our hearts as I shared this profound experience from my grandfather's life. Very little else needed to be said because this small group of faithful people also knew in their own way that Jesus Christ is the Son of God and that He is our Savior and our Redeemer. We all knew that with greater faith in Him, we could reach our goal.

During that same day, family after family came to my office with money, making personal sacrifices that were far beyond what I ever would have asked of them. By eight o'clock that evening, the ward clerk had written receipts for a little more than thirty thousand dollars.

Sacrifice truly brought forth the blessings of heaven to the members of our ward. Never have I lived among people who were more united, more caring, more concerned for one another than these ward members were when making their greatest sacrifices. In the midst of this effort, the sick of our ward were healed through priesthood blessings. The young men set their goals to be fully worthy to serve missions, and most of them did. The young women resolved to settle for nothing but a worthy temple marriage. Sisters of the Relief Society found great joy in rendering compassionate service to others, and home teaching and visiting teaching were completed every month in the spirit of joy and service. In the midst of our greatest sacrifice, our ward members bonded together in a Zion-like spirit of gospel love and service.

WITNESSES OF GOD

Sacrifice is a demonstration of pure love. It is also a clear manifestation of our willingness to "stand as witnesses of God at all times and in all things, and in all places" (Mosiah 18:9). The degree of our love for and commitment to the Lord and His gospel can be measured by what we are willing to sacrifice for Him and for His children. Our Lord and Savior Jesus Christ manifested the supreme example of this loving witness. His life and ministry established a pattern for us to follow. His divine mission culminated in a supreme act of love as He allowed His life to be sacrificed for us. Having power over life and death, He chose to submit himself to pain, ridicule, and suffering and offered His life as a ransom for our sins. Because of His love, He suffered in both body and spirit to a degree beyond our comprehension and took upon Himself our sins. Through His personal sacrifice, He provided a way for us to have our sins forgiven if we repent. Through Him we can find our way back into the presence of our Heavenly Father. The Atonement, therefore, is Christ's ultimate witness of His Divine Sonship and His total commitment to His Father and to His Father's eternal plan for mankind's happiness and peace.

The sacrifice He requires of us is "a broken heart and a contrite spirit" that can lead us to change through repentance. When we finally experience this "mighty change in [our] hearts" and are "spiritually . . . born of God" and receive "his image in [our] countenances" (Alma 5:14), our behaviors are naturally influenced. Our belief in Christ and our acceptance of Him as our Savior is clearly manifest in the way we choose to live our lives. As Alma said, we are "desirous to come into the fold of God, and to be called his people, and are willing to bear one another's burdens, that they may be light;

"Yea, and are willing to mourn with those that mourn; yea, and comfort those that stand in need of comfort, and to stand as witnesses of God at all times and in all things, and in all places that ye may be in, even until death, that ye may be redeemed of God, and be numbered with those of the first resurrection, that ye may have eternal life" (Mosiah 18:8–9).

Indeed, we covenant in the waters of baptism to "stand as witnesses of God at all times and in all things, and in all places." We often think of standing as a witness in terms of standing before congregations and bearing testimony or standing on street corners and shouting our witness to the world. And though such things are important in their time and place, the most important way in which we stand as witnesses of God is in the choices we make every day of our lives. We stand as witnesses of God when we choose to pray and study the scriptures with our families and to pay our tithing, fully and completely, without looking for spiritual loopholes. We stand as witnesses of God when we attend our church meetings, when we serve faithfully and diligently in our callings, when we home teach and visit teach with full purpose of heart, when we avoid off-color stories and crude language, when we walk out of a vulgar movie, when we turn off an offensive television program, when we avoid the misuse of the Internet, when we say no to drugs, alcohol, and tobacco. It may not always be easy, convenient, or politically correct to stand for truth and right, but it is always the right thing to do. Always.

Joseph F. Smith was nineteen when he returned from his

mission in Hawaii. As he traveled from California to his home
in Utah, he was confronted one morning by a "wagon load of
profane drunks . . . shooting their guns, yelling wildly, and curs-
ing the Mormons." One of the drunks, "waving a pistol, came
toward the [camp]fire. . . . Although the missionary was terrified,
he felt it would be unwise and useless to run . . . , and so he
advanced toward the gunman as if he found nothing out of the
ordinary in his conduct. 'Are you a —— —— Mormon?' the
stranger demanded. Mustering all the composure he could,
Joseph answered evenly while looking the man straight in the
eye, 'Yes, siree; dyed in the wool; true blue, through and
through.' Almost stunned by this wholly unexpected response,
the gunman stopped, dropped his hands to his sides, and, after
looking incredulously at Joseph for a moment, said in a sub-
dued tone, 'Well, you are the —— pleasantest man I ever
met! Shake. I am glad to see a fellow stand for his convictions.'
So saying, he turned and walked away" (Gibbons, *Joseph F.
Smith,* 43–44).

STANDING FOR TRUTH AND RIGHT

As followers of Christ, we have a sacred duty always to stand
for truth and right. Being a Christian, being spiritually born of
God, isn't a Sunday-only thing. Nor is it limited to our Church-
related service and associations. For example, every day our
neighborhoods and communities desperately need our support
and our commitment to safety and law and order. Crime, in all
its pervasive manifestations, is a serious worldwide evil and a
moral problem about which Church leaders have great concern.
The social, economic, and moral costs of crime are incalculable.
It is no respecter of race, religion, nationality, age, culture, or
socioeconomic status.

The Book of Mormon teaches that secret combinations
engaged in crime present a serious challenge not just to individuals and families but to entire civilizations. Among today's

secret combinations are gangs, drug cartels, and organized crime families. The secret combinations of our day function much like the Gadianton robbers functioned in Book of Mormon times. They have secret signs and code words. They participate in secret rites and initiation ceremonies. Among their purposes are to "murder, and plunder, and steal, and commit whoredoms and all manner of wickedness, contrary to the laws of their country and also the laws of their God" (Helaman 6:23).

If we are not careful, today's secret combinations can obtain power and influence just as quickly and just as completely as they did in Book of Mormon times. Do you remember the pattern? The secret combinations began among the "more wicked part" of society but eventually "seduced the more part of the righteous" until the whole society was polluted (Helaman 6:38).

Today's young people, just like those "of the rising generation" in the Book of Mormon (Mosiah 26:1), are most susceptible to the influence of gangs. Our young men and young women see it all around them. An entire subculture celebrates contemporary gangs and their criminal conduct with music, clothing styles, language, attitudes, and behaviors. Many of you have watched as trendy friends have embraced the style as something that was "fashionable" and "cool," only to be dragged into the subculture because of their identification with the gangs. We've all heard the tragic stories of unsuspecting "wanna-bees" who have been victimized by gangs simply because they were wearing the wrong color in the wrong neighborhood.

The Book of Mormon teaches that the devil is the "author of all sin" and the "founder" of secret combinations (Helaman 6:30; 2 Nephi 26:22). He uses secret combinations, including gangs, "from generation to generation according as he can get hold upon the hearts of the children of men" (Helaman 6:30). His purpose is to destroy individuals, families, communities, and nations (2 Nephi 9:9). To a degree, he was successful during Book of Mormon times. And he is having far too much success today. That's why it is so important for us as followers of Christ to take a firm stand for truth and right by doing what we can to help keep our communities safe.

Several years before Christ came to the American continent, the Lamanites exercised such great faith and courage that they completely destroyed the influence of the Gadianton robbers in their society by "preach[ing] the word of God among . . . them" (Helaman 6:37). We are now in a similar position to "stand as witnesses of God" by setting an example, keeping Church standards, and sharing our testimony with those around us.

The Savior has promised that if we will "keep all the commandments and covenants by which [we] are bound . . . [He] will cause the heavens to shake for [our] good, and Satan shall tremble and Zion shall rejoice upon the hills and flourish" (D&C 35:24). He has even promised that the day will come when, "because of the righteousness of his people, Satan [will have] no power" over the hearts of men (1 Nephi 22:26).

As a Church, we recognize that the gospel of Jesus Christ, with its saving truths and teachings, provides the most effective preventative and rehabilitative assistance in overcoming criminal behavior. Parents bear the first and greatest responsibility to teach their children principles of gospel living and good citizenship. There are, however, those who have little or no support at home. We need to be aware of them and do all we can to bless their lives. They need positive role models who demonstrate integrity by honoring their covenants and keeping their promises.

To you who are parents and youth leaders: please remember that all young men and young women have a great need to feel loved, respected, and valued, and to succeed in ways that will help them gain a sense of confidence and self-worth. Appropriate and uplifting activities should be planned that will provide a safe and wholesome environment in which our youth and their nonmember friends can strengthen one another and draw closer to the Savior. Leaders should always be careful, however, that activities do not draw young people from their homes without parental approval and involvement.

We should also support the efforts of individuals, organizations, communities, and governments to assist them and help prevent crime. We should work within our respective legal and judicial systems to enact and enforce laws that provide necessary protection against criminals while ensuring essential rights and freedoms. And we should volunteer to support and assist government leaders in promoting programs designed to protect and strengthen families and communities.

To you who are still in your youth: please know that we understand how difficult it can be to set a good example among your peers and associates. Many of you find yourselves on the front lines in the battle against those who intend to do things that are morally wrong. I firmly believe that there are certain things we cannot do if we are to stand for truth and right. President Gordon B. Hinckley has urged us to respect our bodies and not inflict permanent damage on them with tattoos and body piercings, reminding us that "the temple of God is holy, which temple ye are" (1 Corinthians 3:17). It is not possible, at any age, to listen to vulgar lyrics, watch movies filled with sexual innuendo, tamper with pornography on the Internet (or anywhere else), take the name of the Lord in vain, wear revealing clothing, compromise in any way the law of chastity, or disregard the values of true manhood and womanhood, and expect the Holy Ghost to remain with you. Whenever anyone participates in those kinds of activities, it should not be a surprise if feelings of loneliness, discouragement, and unworthiness follow. Do not make the choice to go it alone rather than have the Spirit of the Lord to guide, to protect, to prompt, to warn, and to fill you with peace. Repent if you need to so that your life reflects your love for our Heavenly Father and the Savior.

WHITTLING AND WHISTLING

It is sometimes hard to stand for truth and right, yet we need to be positive examples if we are to help others find a better way. Thankfully, we can draw strength from those who have gone before us. Although the road they walked may have been different from the road we walk today, the courage required to be faithful is similar, and their experiences are instructive.

As a boy growing up in Nauvoo, George Q. Cannon learned to cope with those who would do harm to others. Remember, this was a time when the Church was experiencing continued persecution. Usually, strangers in town were there either as new converts to join with the Saints or as enemies wishing to cause trouble for Church leaders. Brother Cannon described how he and a group of boys his age did their part to defend the Saints against potential troublemakers:

"It was . . . a common practice . . . when engaged in conversation or in making a bargain, to take out . . . pocket knives and commence whittling; frequently . . . accompanying the whittling by whistling. No person could object, therefore, to the practices of whittling and whistling. Many of the boys of the city had each a large bowie knife made, and when a man came to town who was known to be a villain, and there for evil purposes, a few of them would get together, and go where the obnoxious person was, and having previously provided themselves with pine shingles, would commence whittling. The presence of a number of boys, each [harmlessly] whittling . . . was not a sight to escape the notice of a stranger. . . . His first [reaction] . . . would be to . . . ask what this meant. The boys would make no reply, but with grave faces, keep up their [harmless] whistling. What could the man do? If he was armed, he could shoot, but the resolute expression of the boys' faces and the gleaming knives would convince him that discretion was the better part of valor. The most we ever knew them to do was to stand for a while and curse and threaten . . . then they would walk off, followed by a troop of boys vigorously whittling and whistling" (in Flake, *George Q. Cannon*, 23–24).

I'm not suggesting that we begin issuing bowie knives to our deacons, but I am suggesting that George Q. Cannon and his youthful associates exhibited great courage and faith by their actions. They saw something that needed to be done, and they did it safely within the context of what was appropriate for the times. I'm impressed by their willingness to take a stand against the wicked intentions of others.

Dealing with crime in our communities is very complex; however, there are some simple things we can do in our day to prevent others from drifting toward gangs and crime. We can avoid the temptation to be cliquish at school or at church. All of us can refrain from finding fault or alienating anyone by our words or actions. Nothing is more hurtful than to feel left out or made fun of. Therefore, we must never do anything that may drive others towards being accepted by a gang because they feel rejected by us. Many new families are moving in among us. Reach out the hand of friendship and make everyone feel welcome and secure in our neighborhoods whether or not they feel any inclination toward investigating the Church. Guard against spreading rumors or saying unkind things or allowing anything to occur that may hurt another. Make friends with your neighbors. Watch out for each other. Help build a spirit of unity, peace, and love in our neighborhoods.

These may seem like small things, but I assure you they may be every bit as effective in keeping people away from evil and crime as whittling and whistling did in the days of Nauvoo. True friendship may well be the best thing that we can do to help reach those who may be drifting towards unsafe and morally damaging activities and counterfeit forms of belonging. It may also be the simplest, most direct way of standing as witnesses of God.

There are countless stories that could be told of bright,

talented men and women in the Church who have influenced for good the lives of others through their righteous example. Unfortunately, there are also stories of those who fell short of their potential because they were unwilling to take such a stand for truth and right. Some have rationalized their bad choices, saying that we all make mistakes. You must understand that there is a big difference between an honest mistake made in a moment of spiritual weakness and a willful decision to disobey persistently the commandments of God. Those who deliberately choose to violate God's commandments or ignore the standards of the Church, even when promising themselves and others that someday they will be strong enough to repent, are stepping onto a dangerously slippery slope upon which many have lost their spiritual footing. Though it is true that some young people, and some not so young, have made remarkable recoveries from sin through the difficult process of repentance, the sad reality is that others have lost their way because of the paths they have chosen to follow. Stay away from those things that would weaken your ability to stand for truth or cause the Spirit to withdraw.

These are difficult times in which we are living. In some respects, it is perhaps the most challenging age of all time. We are aware of that. We are also aware that God has reserved some of His strongest spirit children for these perilous days. Although God's laws and standards of right and wrong are under attack at every turn, we are prepared to make a valiant stand for truth and right. Let us stand shoulder to shoulder and as followers of Christ do what we can to make this a better, safer, and happier world. Let us be "witnesses of God at all times and in all things, and in all places" (Mosiah 18:9).

As we do so, and as we experience that mighty change of heart to which Alma referred (Alma 5:12), not only do we have the privilege of helping others find Christ in the light of our witness but we are also spared the heartache, pain, and frustration that come from making wrong choices. In these final hours as the time of Christ's triumphal return approaches, we need to stay as close as possible to the influence of the Spirit if we are to safely complete our journey here.

No Man Knows

Toward the end of the Savior's ministry, His disciples came to Him with several questions, all centered on one key prophetic event: "Tell us, when shall these things be? And what shall be the sign of thy coming, and of the end of the world?" (Matthew 24:3). Two thousand years ago, Christ's followers were concerned about that. Every generation of believers since then, I think, has been concerned about the last days to one degree or another. So the Lord's response to His disciples is meaningful to all of us. To the first question—"When shall these things be?"—He replied, "Take heed that no man deceive you." That is very significant, "for many shall come in my name, saying, I am Christ; and shall deceive many. And ye shall hear of wars and rumours of wars: see that ye be not troubled: for all these things must come to pass, but the end is not yet. For nation shall rise against nation, and kingdom against kingdom: and there shall be famines, and pestilences, and earthquakes, in divers places" (Matthew 24:4–7).

We need only listen to the news to know that the earth is rumbling, and earthquakes are occurring in "divers places." We read almost daily that somewhere in the world there has been a hurricane, a tornado, a volcanic eruption, or extensive flooding. Can we use scientific data surrounding these natural disasters to extrapolate that the Second Coming is likely to occur during the next few years, or the next decade, or the next century? Not really. I have been called as one of the Apostles to be a special witness of Christ in these exciting yet trying times, and I do not know when He is going to come again. As far as I know, none of my Brethren in the Council of the Twelve or even in the First

Presidency knows. I would humbly suggest to you that if we do not know, then nobody knows, no matter how compelling their arguments or how reasonable their calculations. The Savior said that "of that day and hour knoweth no man, no, not the angels of heaven, but my Father only" (Matthew 24:36). I believe when the Lord says "no man" knows, it really means that no man knows. In 1844 Joseph Smith declared: "Jesus Christ never did reveal to any man the precise time that He would come. Go and read the scriptures, and you cannot find anything that specifies the exact hour He would come; and all that say so are false teachers" (*History of the Church,* 6:254). You should be extremely wary of anyone who claims to be an exception to divine decree.

But though the exact timing of the Second Coming remains in doubt, there is no question that scriptural prophecy relative to that momentous and sacred event is being fulfilled, sometimes in remarkable ways.

BEWARE OF FALSE CHRISTS

Continuing to speak of His own Second Coming, Jesus said, "Then shall many be offended, and shall betray one another, and shall hate one another. And many false prophets shall rise, and shall deceive many" (Matthew 24:10–11).

You may not be aware of it, but there are "false prophets" rising within and without the Church. They believe they have had revelations and that they know something the First Presidency and the Twelve Apostles don't know. You need to be very careful of such people. If you are ever approached by anyone who claims special authority or revelation from God outside the sustained priesthood authority, turn and run from them as fast as you can. The Savior said that in the last days even the very elect could be pulled away from the truth by such false prophets.

Some false prophets have arisen among the congregations of the Church. A few groups have drifted away from the gospel under the direction of those who claim to have received special instruction through personal revelation, and some have declared themselves prophets. I know of one group that is led by a bright, capable, articulate young man who claims to have received a revelation that he is the prophet and that he was called of God to establish the true church. Sadly, those who have chosen to follow such individuals are in turn led directly away from the principles of truth and righteousness. Perhaps that is why it is so interesting to me that when the Master was asked about the sign of His Second Coming and the end of the world, he responded by warning His listeners to beware of false prophets.

The Love of Many Shall Wax Cold

The Savior's next comment, found in Matthew 24:12, is similarly interesting: "Because iniquity shall abound, the love of many shall wax cold."

Think about what that means. Today, we are living in a society in which many men and women see no real purpose in marriage. Relationships in which people just live together without legally and lawfully making a formal commitment to each other through marriage are escalating at an ever-increasing rate. In the United States, the birth rate of children to unwed mothers is at an all-time high. So is the divorce rate.

In an article entitled "Redeeming Our Time," William J. Bennett, former United States Secretary of Education, noted:

"During the same thirty-year period [1960–1990], there was a 560 percent increase in violent crime; more than a 400 percent increase in illegitimate births; a quadrupling in divorces; a tripling of the percentage of children living in single-parent homes; more than a 200 percent increase in the teenage suicide rate; and a drop of 75 points in the average SAT scores of high school students.

"Today, 30 percent of all births . . . are illegitimate. By the end of the decade, according to the most reliable projections, 40 percent of all American births . . . will occur out of wedlock."

MEDIA INFLUENCES ON THE PURE IN HEART

With so little of long-lasting, fully committed love in the world today, one would think we could turn to entertainment mediums to find a better, happier, more satisfying model for living. After all, history indicates there have always been storytellers and dramatists who encouraged their audiences with stories of a better world, where maidens are fair, where princes are charming, and where everyone always lives happily ever after. Unfortunately, current entertainment forms tend to portray life even uglier and harsher than it really is. Movie critic Michael Medved laments the demise of larger-than-life heroes on film and television programs, claiming that we are now living in an age of smaller-than-life antiheroes.

Sadly, one doesn't have to look far to find all manner of violence, ugliness, and illicit sexuality coming at us over the public airwaves. At the same time, wholesome, clean, uplifting, inspiring programs are few and far between. Hollywood and the television industry must be held accountable for their influence on America's social landscape, and I believe that influence is considerable. I believe you cannot watch on film as people are gunned down in cold blood, in living color, and not have it affect the attitudes and thoughts of those who see it. I believe you cannot continually portray human sexuality as just another physical appetite that has to be satisfied—whenever and with whomever (including those of the same gender) the urge strikes—without diminishing respect for God and His commandments. And I believe that the desensitizing effect of such media abuses on the hearts and souls of those who are exposed to them result in a partial fulfillment of the Savior's statement that "because iniquity shall abound, the love of many shall wax cold" (Matthew 24:12).

Standing as witnesses of God "at all times, and in all places," therefore, even means being careful in our choices of what we watch and what we read. Pornography is rampant and is absolutely, totally, completely destructive. One simply cannot stand as a witness for God while under its influence, no matter how much you may try to convince yourself that you can. God's image cannot be reflected in the countenance of one who chooses to follow the path of pornography.

Not long ago I was assigned by the First Presidency to interview a man who had been excommunicated from the Church for adultery. It had required eight years for him to work his way through the long and sometimes painful process of reinstatement in the Church, and now he was sitting before me in an interview to determine his worthiness for a possible restoration of his priesthood and temple blessings. I asked him this question: "My dear brother, looking back on this traumatic time in your life, how did it happen?"

Tears began to flow freely down his cheeks as he tried to respond. At last he was able to speak. "Brother Ballard," he said, "it all started the day I picked up a pornographic magazine in the barbershop. It was the first time in my life I had ever seen anything like that, and it intrigued me. I wanted to see more and more. Then I wanted to see things that were progressively more explicit. And then it wasn't enough to just look at pictures—I wanted to actually participate in some of the activities I was looking at. Eventually, I was untrue to my wife and my family, and unfaithful to covenants I had made with my Heavenly Father in His holy house."

The man continued through his tears: "I'm not trying to shift blame for the choices I made. I knew better than to do what I did, and I alone am responsible for my sins. But there's no question in my mind that exposure to pornography played a significant role in my spiritual decline."

Then he made this humble request: "When you talk to the

brethren of the Church, please warn them. Please tell them to be careful about the things they read and watch."

I'm also extending that same warning to all members of the Church—male and female. Please stand for truth and right in your entertainment choices. Some of the things that are being shown in our theaters and broadcast into our homes via television and videos and over the Internet are insidious and dangerous. Rather than falling within the scriptural admonition to seek after that which is "virtuous, lovely, or of good report or praiseworthy" (Article of Faith 13), they are more clearly described in Moroni 7, in which the prophet Mormon teaches that "whatsoever thing persuadeth men to do evil, and believe not in Christ, and deny him, and serve not God . . . is of the devil" (Moroni 7:17).

I am aware that some may think they know better than I do about this subject. They may argue their case based on artistic merit or that "everyone is seeing it," or they may insist that they are not one of those people who will be influenced one way or the other by on-screen sex or violence. To them I have only one question: Are you going to stand for truth and right, or not? That is the real issue here. If you choose to read anything that contains material that is contrary to the moral standards of the Church, then you are placing yourself and your own wisdom above the counsel of God's prophets—a course of action that would indeed be very unwise. As soon as people begin to think they know better than God or His oracles, or that counsel given doesn't apply to them, they are stepping onto that slippery slope that has claimed far too many victims already. It takes faith—real faith, unequivocal and unreserved—to accept and attempt to live prophetic counsel even when you don't completely understand it. Such simple faith has the power to guide you safely through every challenge you may face in your life, and it places you as a witness of God through humble, sincere obedience, maintaining another vital link in your gospel chain.

A few years ago, I spoke at the funeral of one of my righteous senior missionaries. As I thought about his life, I realized that he had remained faithful and true because he had a believing heart. His willingness to believe and to live the gospel made of my friend a beacon of light and truth, a magnificent witness of God. He was surely prepared to meet the Savior as a "good and faithful servant" (Matthew 25:21).

The Father of All Lies

Of course, Lucifer doesn't want us to feel or exhibit that kind of faith, and so he tries to make us feel uncomfortable with obedience. He plants defiance in our hearts and an ability to justify and rationalize our actions, subtly convincing us that it is possible to live the spirit of the law even if we are not keeping the commandments. Eventually, he can make it seem wrong—or at least politically incorrect—to obey, branding it with such derogatory labels as "blind faith."

We must never forget this about Lucifer: he is a liar. He is the father of all lies and has been from the beginning. He was cast out of Heavenly Father's premortal kingdom because of his disobedience. Now he and those who followed him have one goal, one eternal commitment that has never changed from the time of the war in heaven until the present day. Their sole purpose is to make you and me as miserable as they are, and the best way for them to accomplish that is to entice us into disobedience. Although there are all kinds of misery in this world, the only kind that is eternal is misery of the soul; and that kind of misery is centered in sin and transgression. Be careful; stay morally clean in mind and body. Do not compromise the standards of chastity. Stand for truth and right in your personal lives and in all your associations with others.

When we are not doing what we know we ought to be doing and when we are not living the way we know we ought to live, we have a tendency to be unhappy. And make no mistake about it: We know when we are not doing what we ought to do because every one of us has a conscience. We are born with the light of Christ, and we know instinctively what is right and what is wrong when it comes to our personal behavior. It offends the Spirit when we allow ourselves and our values and standards to be manipulated by atheistic propaganda in behalf of Satan's lies.

Consider the following words from the Apostle Paul in connection with much of what we see and hear in contemporary media:

"This know also, that in the last days perilous times shall come.

"For men shall be lovers of their own selves, covetous, boasters, proud, blasphemers, disobedient to parents, unthankful, unholy,

"Without natural affection, trucebreakers, false accusers, incontinent, fierce, despisers of those that are good,

"Traitors, heady, high-minded, lovers of pleasures more than lovers of God;

"Having a form of godliness, but denying the power thereof: from such turn away.

"For of this sort are they which creep into houses, and lead captive silly women laden with sins, led away with divers lusts.

"Ever learning, and never able to come to the knowledge of the truth" (2 Timothy 3:1-7).

It sounds almost as if Paul were doing some late-night channel surfing, doesn't it? I'm kidding about that, of course, but some of what Paul describes here does sound like it's right out of prime time.

"Men shall be lovers of their own selves" . . . "boasters" . . . "proud" . . . "blasphemers" . . . "disobedient to parents" . . . "unthankful" . . . "unholy" . . . "despisers of those that are good" . . . "lovers of pleasures more than lovers of God" . . . "silly women laden with sins" . . . "led away with divers lusts" . . . "ever learning, and never able to come to the knowledge of the truth."

I especially like Paul's warning about that which can "creep into houses." Does any of this sound familiar?

Now, please don't misunderstand. I'm not trying to say that all of film or television or publishing or music is evil, because you and I both know that is simply not true. There is much that is good in the media, and it can be a wondrous and marvelous thing and a blessing to our lives. But some of it is evil; there can be no other word to describe it.

WHO'S ON THE LORD'S SIDE?

Because of the restoration of the gospel, we live in a time when so many of the teachings of God have been made known—when the gifts and blessings of the priesthood and the doctrines of all previous dispensations have been given to us. There never has been a greater time than this to be living on the earth. But we also must never forget that Satan and his fallen followers are active and doing all they can to thwart God's plan and destroy the faith of His children. We are at war. The forces of evil are marshalled against truth and right. This is a continuation of the same war that raged in the premortal world.

Lucifer and his followers are committed to their evil direction. Our Heavenly Father and His Beloved Son, Jesus Christ, have a plan, and they have delegated to us as members of Their Church the responsibility of representing Them at the battle front, which stretches all the way around the world and on both sides of the veil. This is the time—right now, today—to be valiant in standing for truth and right with the image of God on our countenance. Will we be faithful "witnesses of God at all times and in all things, and in all places"? Will we be true? Or will we succumb to the adversarial pressure that rages all around us in hideous forms that are appealingly disguised under robes of fad, fashion, expediency, desirability, and political correctness?

In many ways our situation is not unlike the situation Moses encountered when he came down from conversing with the

Lord on the Holy Mount. He had just come from the presence of the Lord, receiving from Him the commandments that should serve as the Law for His children. But Moses found that in his absence his followers had been unable to make good choices. Even his beloved brother, Aaron, had been unable to stand for truth and right and had fashioned of gold an idol for the people to worship.

The scriptures tell us Moses was angry, and I think I can understand that. It's frustrating to watch people you love make bad choices. So he took the stone tablets upon which the Lord had written His law, and he cast them to the ground and broke them.

"Then Moses stood in the gate of the camp, and said, Who is on the Lord's side?" (Exodus 32:26). His people had to make a choice.

I never read that passage without thinking of the words of the hymn:

> Who's on the Lord's side? Who?
> Now is the time to show.
> We ask it fearlessly:
> Who's on the Lord's side? Who?
>
> We serve the living God,
> And want his foes to know
> That, if but few, we're great;
> Who's on the Lord's side? Who?
>
> The stone cut without hands
> To fill the earth must grow.
> Who'll help to roll it on?
> Who's on the Lord's side? Who?
>
> The powers of earth and hell
> In rage direct the blow

That's aimed to crush the work;
Who's on the Lord's side? Who?

Truth, life and liberty,
Freedom from death and woe,
Are stakes we're fighting for;
Who's on the Lord's side? Who?
                    (*Hymns,* no. 260)

It's a compelling question, isn't it? It may seem almost rhetorical, because of course we all want to be on the Lord's side. But the fact is, there isn't a more important question that any of us will have to answer throughout the period of our mortal lives. We may want to be on the Lord's side, and we may feel that with all of our hearts. Are we prepared to pay the price for such discipleship? Are we willing to take a stand for truth and right? Is this gospel link polished to such a high gloss that we are ready to "stand as witnesses of God at all times, and in all places"? And are we ready to do so—right now, today?

CHAPTER 7

SERVING OTHERS

Sometimes we become so involved in the process of daily living that we do not seek out opportunities to serve others. Neglecting this link in our anchor chain will make it susceptible to the rust and corrosion that can weaken the whole chain that binds us to our faith in the Lord Jesus Christ.

It is difficult for those of us who weren't there to fully appreciate the mood in Carthage Jail during the hours leading up to the martyrdom of Joseph and Hyrum Smith. It is clear from the historical record that Joseph sensed his mortal ministry was coming to an end. Two or three days earlier, some of his brethren had convinced him not to flee for safety, as he was inclined to do, but to turn himself over to local authorities and answer the charges against him. They were sure these charges would be proven false just as they had been many times before. In deciding to return to Nauvoo, the Prophet told them: "I am going like a lamb to the slaughter" (D&C 135:4).

Doubtless this thought hung heavily in Carthage Jail that June morning as Joseph and Hyrum awaited their fate. Willard Richards and John Taylor were visitors in their cell. It is significant to me that at this particular moment in time, with death looming imminently, Brother Taylor sang "A Poor Wayfaring Man of Grief," a hymn based on the Savior's teaching that "inasmuch as ye have done it unto one of the least of these my brethren, ye have done it unto me" (Matthew 25:40). Consider James Montgomery's words in that context:

> A poor wayfaring Man of grief
> Hath often crossed me on my way,
> Who sued so humbly for relief
> That I could never answer nay.
> I had not pow'r to ask his name,
> Where-to he went or whence he came;
> Yet there was something in his eye
> That won my love; I knew not why.
>
> Once, when my scanty meal was spread,
> He entered; not a word he spake,
> Just perishing for want of bread.
> I gave him all; he blessed it, brake,
> And ate, but gave me part again.
> Mine was an angel's portion then,
> For while I fed with eager haste,
> The crust was manna to my taste.
>
> I spied him where a fountain burst
> Clear from the rock; his strength was gone.
> The heedless water mocked his thirst;
> He heard it, saw it hurrying on.
> I ran and raised the suff'rer up;
> Thrice from the stream he drained my cup,
> Dipped and returned it running o'er;
> I drank and never thirsted more.
>
> 'Twas night; the floods were out; it blew
> A winter hurricane aloof.

I heard his voice abroad and flew
To bid him welcome to my roof.
I warmed and clothed and cheered my guest
And laid him on my couch to rest;
Then made the earth my bed, and seemed
In Eden's garden while I dreamed.

Stript, wounded, beaten nigh to death,
I found him by the highway side.
I roused his pulse, brought back his breath,
Revived his spirit, and supplied
Wine, oil, refreshment—he was healed.
I had myself a wound concealed,
But from that hour forgot the smart,
And peace bound up my broken heart.

In pris'n I saw him next, condemned
To meet a traitor's doom at morn.
The tide of lying tongues I stemmed,
And honored him 'mid shame and scorn.
My friendship's utmost zeal to try,
He asked if I for him would die.
The flesh was weak; my blood ran chill,
But my free spirit cried, "I will!"

Then in a moment to my view
The stranger started from disguise.
The tokens in his hands I knew;
The Savior stood before mine eyes.
He spake, and my poor name he named,
"Of me thou hast not been ashamed.
These deeds shall thy memorial be;
Fear not, thou didst them unto me."

(Hymns, no. 29)

After Brother Taylor finished singing the song, Joseph asked him to sing it again. I can't help but think that Joseph and Hyrum both found peace and comfort in the song's message, knowing they had done their best to serve others and they could face their Master with "a conscience void of offense towards God, and towards all men" (D&C 135:4).

It is interesting—and I don't think at all coincidental—that the Lord Jesus Christ was similarly focused on compassionate service as he neared the end of His mortal ministry. And why not? He was about to undertake the most powerfully compassionate service ever performed in the history of mankind as He walked through the excruciatingly painful steps and processes of the Atonement. It seems natural and appropriate that His last instructions to His disciples would include counsel on the need to serve one another, even as He was about to serve them in ways they could not comprehend.

After they had eaten their Passover meal, "he riseth from supper, and laid aside his garments; and took a towel, and girded himself. After that he poureth water into a bason, and began to wash the disciples' feet, and to wipe them with the towel wherewith he was girded" (John 13:4-5).

Consider the powerful simplicity of that extraordinary moment. The Savior of the world is on bended knee, humbly washing the dust of the road from feet caked with the grime of miles and miles of travel. This was a task for the lowliest of household servants; certainly not befitting Him who had so recently made a triumphant entry into Jerusalem, as believers hailed Him as one who had real and lasting authority. Peter couldn't get past the incongruity of the scene, and he had to be persuaded to allow Jesus to wash his feet.

"So after he had washed their feet, and had taken his garments, and was set down again, he said unto them, Know ye what I have done to you?

"Ye call me Master and Lord: and ye say well; for so I am.

"If I then, your Lord and Master, have washed your feet; ye also ought to wash one another's feet.

"For I have given you an example, that ye should do as I have done to you.

"Verily, verily, I say unto you, The servant is not greater than his lord; neither he that is sent greater than he that sent him.

"If ye know these things, happy are ye if ye do them" (John 13:12-17).

SERVICE TO MANKIND

I can't help but think that if this lesson was important enough to the Savior that He would spend His last precious mortal moments trying to teach it to His Apostles, it must also be of paramount importance to us in our continuing search for happiness and peace. Those who love the Lord and seek to follow Him understand that His very work and glory depend upon bringing to pass "the immortality and eternal life of man" (Moses 1:39). Therefore, it naturally follows that "when ye are in the service of your fellow beings ye are only in the service of your God" (Mosiah 2:17).

In teaching His Apostles about the Resurrection and the Judgment, the Savior made it clear that service to mankind was among the critical factors in this process. He even used a parable to illustrate the point:

"When the Son of man shall come in his glory, and all the holy angels with him, then shall he sit upon the throne of his glory:

"And before him shall be gathered all nations: and he shall separate them one from another, as a shepherd divideth his sheep from the goats:

"And he shall set the sheep on the right hand, but the goats on the left.

"Then shall the King say unto them on his right hand,

Come, ye blessed of my Father, inherit the kingdom prepared for you from the foundation of the world:

"For I was an hungred, and ye gave me meat: I was thirsty, and ye gave me drink: I was a stranger, and ye took me in:

"Naked, and ye clothed me: I was sick, and ye visited me: I was in prison, and ye came unto me.

"Then shall the righteous answer him, saying, Lord, when saw we thee an hungred, and fed thee? or thirsty, and gave thee drink?

"When saw we thee a stranger, and took thee in? or naked, and clothed thee?

"Or when saw we thee sick, or in prison, and came unto thee?

"And the King shall answer and say unto them, Verily I say unto you, Inasmuch as ye have done it unto one of the least of these my brethren, ye have done it unto me" (Matthew 25:31–40).

To further illustrate the point, the Lord continued the parable to talk about what would happen to those who choose not to serve "the least of these":

"Then shall he say also unto them on the left hand, Depart from me, ye cursed, into everlasting fire, prepared for the devil and his angels:

"For I was an hungred, and ye gave me no meat: I was thirsty, and ye gave me no drink:

"I was a stranger, and ye took me not in: naked, and ye clothed me not: sick, and in prison, and ye visited me not.

"Then shall they also answer him, saying, Lord, when saw we thee an hungred, or athirst, or a stranger, or naked, or sick, or in prison, and did not minister unto thee?

"Then shall he answer them, saying, Verily I say unto you, Inasmuch as ye did it not to one of the least of these, ye did it not to me.

"And these shall go away into everlasting punishment: but the righteous into life eternal" (Matthew 25:41–46).

While it is tempting to apply the parable specifically to Church service—especially home teaching and visiting teaching, which seem to have such direct application to ministering to those in need—I don't believe the Savior's scope was in any way limited by ecclesiastical connection. He regards all of humanity with equal love and tenderness, and I am confident He would have us extend our Christian vision beyond the ward and the stake. The Church is extensively involved in humanitarian service throughout the world, and the members of the Church are becoming more aware of our obligation and opportunity to "the least of these"—wherever and whoever they might be.

"Charity Never Faileth"

"Charity, or love, is the greatest principle in existence," said President Joseph F. Smith. "If we can lend a helping hand to the oppressed, if we can aid those who are despondent and in sorrow, if we can uplift and ameliorate the condition of mankind, it is our mission to do it, it is an essential part of our religion to do it" (Conference Report, April 1917, 4).

President Smith was not unaware of the effect of such charitable service in people's lives, including those who would otherwise be strangers. When he was a young missionary in Hawaii (and please keep in mind that he was a *young* missionary; he was called to serve when just fifteen years of age), he contracted a severe fever and was seriously ill for three months. It was a difficult time for young Joseph. As a child he had lost his father, Hyrum, a victim of mob bullets along with his uncle Joseph Smith. His mother, Mary Fielding Smith, had died when he was thirteen. Fatherless and motherless and alone in a strange land, he struggled through an illness that left him painfully weak. A wonderful Hawaiian woman, Ma Mahuhii, took him in and attended to his needs as lovingly as though he were her own son. He never forgot the effect of that sweet and gentle service on his life.

Years later, he returned to the islands as president of the Church. Bishop Charles W. Nibley, who accompanied President Smith on the journey, shared the following observation:

"As we landed at the wharf in Honolulu, the native Saints were out in great numbers with their wreaths of leis, beautiful flowers of every variety and hue. We were loaded with them, he, or course, more than anyone else. . . . It was a beautiful sight to see the deep-seated love, the even tearful affection, that these people had for him. In the midst of it all I noticed a poor, old, blind woman, tottering under the weight of about ninety years, being led in. She had a few choice bananas in her hand. It was her all—her offering. She was calling, 'Iosepa, Iosepa.' Instantly, when he saw her, he ran to her and clasped her in his arms, hugged her, and kissed her over and over again, patting her on the head saying, 'Mama, Mama, my dear old Mama.'

"And with tears streaming down his cheeks he turned to me and said, 'Charlie, she nursed me when I was a boy, sick and without anyone to care for me. She took me in and was a mother to me.'

"Oh, it was touching . . . It was beautiful to see the great, noble soul in loving, tender remembrance of kindness extended to him more than fifty years before; and the poor old soul who had brought her love offering—a few bananas—it was all she had—to put into the hand of her beloved Iosepa!" ("Reminiscences," in Smith, *Gospel Doctrine,* 519–20).

As the Apostle Paul wrote to the Saints in Corinth:

"Though I speak with the tongues of men and of angels, and have not charity, I am become as sounding brass, or a tinkling cymbal.

"And though I have the gift of prophecy, and understand all mysteries, and all knowledge; and though I have all faith, so that I could remove mountains, and have not charity, I am nothing.

"And though I bestow all my goods to feed the poor, and though I give my body to be burned, and have not charity, it profiteth me nothing. . . .

"Charity never faileth. . . .

"And now abideth faith, hope, charity, these three; but the greatest of these is charity" (1 Corinthians 13:1–3, 8, 13).

SERVICE THROUGH SHARING THE GOSPEL

Let's return to "A Poor Wayfaring Man of Grief." The hymn certainly talks about outward acts of service. Interestingly enough, all of the verses could also speak metaphorically about the greatest service we can perform for others: sharing the gospel message—giving water to the thirsty, clothing the naked, freeing the soul from the prison of ignorance. During His mortal ministry, the Savior used all of these examples as metaphors for "the living water" and "the bread of life" that He brought into the world.

Certainly, there is no greater service we can render in this life than to share the gospel message with those who are sincerely seeking truth. Of course, there are many ways to share the gospel. Many missionaries have proclaimed the gospel as I did during my first mission to England, standing on street corners and preaching at the top of our lungs. This was a great experience and an important character builder, but it wasn't an especially effective way of bringing people to Christ. Far more effective is the sharing that takes place when faithful Latter-day Saints live the gospel in dynamic ways, sending out positive, faith-affirming messages to any and all who experience the power of their example.

Although we should be pleased to testify to the truthfulness of the restored gospel of Jesus Christ to any and all who will hear our message, there are times when all that we can hope to accomplish is to help those who are not members of the Church better understand our basic beliefs. At such times, increasing

understanding is every bit as worthy a goal as increasing con-
versions. Many people know a little about us and are curious
about us but are not ready to change their lifestyle or make eternal commitments. We need to be prepared to teach them in
ways that they can understand and appreciate, even if they are
not prepared as yet to respond to spiritual promptings and to
accept the gospel in their lives.

We often think of Ammon as a great example of missionary
service. You will recall that he prepared the king's heart to
receive God's word by being a faithful servant, protecting the
king's flocks and caring for his horses. King Lamoni was astonished at Ammon's faithfulness, saying, "Surely there has not
been any servant among all my servants that has been so faithful as this man; for even he doth remember all my commandments to execute them" (Alma 18:10). This sincere expression
of love resulted in the conversion of King Lamoni, his family
and his people. Anyone who has read that story knows what far-
reaching impact this had on the Lord's work. We want our missionaries to develop the Ammon spirit by performing regular
meaningful acts of service among the people they've been called
to serve.

While Elder Heber C. Kimball was serving a mission in
Vermont, he baptized twenty souls in a town called Ogdens-
burg. He owed his success in part to a marvelous feat of
strength. One afternoon as a man by the name of Chapin was
grinding his scythe and fixing his cradle to cut a field of wheat,
Heber offered to help and offhandedly declared that he could
rake and bind as fast as Chapin could cut. The surprised
Chapin replied that no living man could do that.

"Never mind, Brother Chapin, it's nearly as easy for me to
do it as to say it," Heber announced.

Elder Kimball's account continues: "The next morning after
the dew had passed off we went into the field, commencing at a
piece of wheat which he said had three acres in it. Said I, 'go

ahead, Brother [Chapin], we'll cut down this piece before dinner.' About the time he took the last clipp of the three acres I had it bound in a bundle before he had hardly a chance to look around, and about that time the horn blew to call us to dinner. We started back to his house; he never spoke or said one word to me, appearing rather confounded. The next Sabbath we had such a congregation of hearers as I had never seen in the United States; for priests and people had come for twenty-five miles distance, to see and hear that 'Mormon' who had performed a thing that had never before been done in that country, for Brother Chapin had proclaimed this occurrence, unknown to me" (Whitney, *Life of Heber C. Kimball,* 96).

PRIMARY MISSIONARIES

Such stories of remarkable missionary service are not limited to the Church's pioneer era. Indeed, they are not limited to adults. Some years ago I was assigned to attend a stake conference in Idaho. When I arrived there, the stake president said, "Brother Ballard, do you trust me?"

I replied, "Well, I like to think that we trust all of our stake presidents. Why do you ask?"

"I would like to have two people speak tomorrow and take part of the time you have assigned me," he said. "They have a marvelous missionary story you will enjoy."

How could I pass up an intriguing suggestion like that? I told him I would trust him to share his time as he saw fit. I'll never forget what I heard from the pulpit the next day when the stake president introduced a nine-year-old girl as a speaker in the conference. They had a platform for her to climb up on so she could tell her story.

"One of the stake high councilors came to our ward Primary and called all of the children to be Primary missionaries," she said in her strong little voice. "So I went home and told my daddy and mommy that I had been called to be a Primary missionary."

Though her father was bishop of her ward, he didn't know what that meant. But she did. She knew that she was supposed to go out and find somebody and bring them into the Church. So she said, "Daddy, I want you to go with me, and we will go meet some people in our ward who aren't members of the Church."

As bishop, her father knew that there were only two families living within the ward boundaries who were not Latter-day Saints, and both of those families had been given ample opportunity to hear the gospel message. The bishop tried to prepare his daughter for rejection, and then he went with her to visit the families. At the home of one family, the mother answered the door. This brave little missionary said, "I am a Primary missionary, and I have come here with my father to ask you to come and have family home evening with our family."

If you could have seen the beautiful, trusting eyes of the little Primary missionary, then you would know why this mother could not resist what was happening and agreed to come.

The nonmember family joined the bishop's family in a family home evening. It was a lovely evening, but it did not prompt any progression toward baptism. Two weeks later our little missionary came home from school just as her mother was taking some banana nut bread from the oven.

"Mommy," she asked, "could I have a loaf of that bread?"

"Well, sure, sweetheart," her mother said. "But what do you want it for?"

"I want to take it to my missionary family," she said.

"I think that's a great idea," her mother said, and she wrapped the loaf, preparing it to be taken to their neighbors.

Once again, our Primary missionary took the lead at the

doorstep. "I have a present for you," she said when the mother came to the door.

"Oh, that's nice, sweetheart," she said.

"But I can't give it to you except on one condition."

"What's that?" she asked.

"That you let the missionaries teach you the gospel."

Touched by the girl's bold sincerity, the mother of the non-member family accepted the challenge. It probably won't surprise you to learn that just a short time later, as a result of the efforts of this dynamic little Primary missionary, the entire family—including father, mother, and three sons—was baptized.

In fact, the newly baptized mother was the second speaker to take some of the stake president's time during that stake conference. She had difficulty speaking because of the emotion she felt as she was expressing her love for her missionary. That was a great teaching moment for a General Authority. One year later, I had the privilege of performing the sealing for that great family in the Idaho Falls Temple. It was a joyous occasion, and a most memorable part of that whole experience occurred after the ceremony in the waiting area of the temple, when father and mother embraced and thanked this special little girl.

If you ask members of this convert family, they will uniformly agree that sharing the gospel is among the greatest acts of service we can perform as disciples of the Savior.

In another instance, the Relief Society and priesthood quorums had been working with a part-member family in the stake but had failed to make progress with the parents. Primary leaders found the answer. Permission was given by the parents for their young daughter to attend Primary. Their one condition was that she had to want to go badly enough to get there on her own. Rides to church would not be provided. Because she had to travel through a rough part of town, the ward council saw to it that someone drove along beside her as she rode an old bicycle to church. Through summer heat, through rain and even snow, she persisted in going to church. One young man, who with his family was assigned to escort her on a snowy morning, was so touched as he watched the commitment of this little girl peddling through the snow and cold that he decided to serve a full-time mission, citing this experience as the turning point in his life. At Christmastime, a family in the ward gave this faithful little girl a new ten-speed bicycle. This softened the hearts of the parents; they too began attending church. The following May this young girl was baptized. What made the baptism even more special was that it was performed by the newest priest in the ward, her recently activated father.

SERVICE IN THE CHURCH

On Thursday morning, 10 October 1985, in the fourth-floor council room of the Salt Lake Temple, I was invited to sit on a small stool placed at the feet of President Spencer W. Kimball, who sat in a chair. With President Kimball's hands on my head and surrounded in a circle by President Gordon B. Hinckley and all the members of the Quorum of the Twelve, I was ordained an Apostle of the Lord Jesus Christ and set apart as a member of the Quorum of the Twelve. It was one of the last priesthood ordinances in which our beloved President Kimball participated prior to his passing, and President Hinckley was voice. I was given a blessing that is a great source of comfort and strength to me to this very day. I was then and am still now overwhelmed with this calling to serve as a special witness of the Lord.

As I have relived this most meaningful experience in my life over and over again, I have asked myself the question that I believe almost everyone asks when called to serve in the Church: "Why me, Lord?" The privilege of serving as a General Authority for most of the past three decades has taken me to many parts of the earth on errands for the Lord. I believe I know as well as anyone in the Church that there are thousands of faithful and devoted men and women who serve the Lord with their whole soul and with great distinction. Knowing as I do that many men are worthy and capable of this sacred calling, the question "Why me?" has had a sobering impact upon my own soul.

I have come to the comforting knowledge that the Lord and my Brethren see in me something that I can do to help the work of the Lord continue to move forward in this calling. That is true for all of us, in any calling we are given through the insight and inspiration of the Holy Spirit. If we take our calling to serve seriously and listen to spiritual promptings and follow them, we can have a significant impact on the work, sometimes in unusual and unforeseen ways.

Years ago I was released as bishop of a ward in Salt Lake City and called to serve as priest quorum advisor. At that time we had more than thirty priests in our ward. Most of them were pretty active, but one young man presented a bit of a challenge. His father was not a member of the Church, and his mother was partially active. As a result, the young man had not been to church for about six or seven years. I went to his home to call on him. He tolerated my visit, but I didn't get very far.

For a few days, I spent a lot of time pondering about this boy and pleading with the Lord in prayer for guidance. The clear impression came that the way to reach him was to go for a ride with him in his Jeep. So I marched over to his house and said, "Why don't you take me for a ride in your Jeep?"

His eyes lit up. "Really, Brother Ballard?" he asked.

"Sure!" I said.

"Well, where do you want to go?"

"I don't care," I responded. "Just anywhere you want to take me."

Now, I probably shouldn't have said that—at least, not to a young man with a Jeep! I probably should have said, "Just take me around the block five times." But I told him to take me wherever he wanted to take me, and he did. We got into the Jeep and strapped ourselves in with everything we could find. He headed right for the hills. He knew how to drive that Jeep. That was the first and only time I have ever been airborne in a four-wheeled vehicle.

It was a Saturday morning, and it was rather dusty. The top was down. I ate enough dust and bounced long enough over rough terrain that by the time we got back my brain was a little addled. As I was getting ready to go home, I said, "I'll pick you up in the morning at 7:45 for priesthood meeting. You be ready."

I didn't even wait for his answer. I just left.

Well, at quarter to eight, I was there. I rang the doorbell, and the boy's father answered. I said, "Would you tell your son I am here to take him to priesthood meeting?"

"He's still in bed," his father said.

"Well, would you get him up and tell him I am out here waiting?" Yes, that's probably a little bold. I blame it on all the dust I had eaten the previous day.

In a few minutes, my new friend's mother came to the door. I said, "Would you please wake up your son?" Then I added, "If you don't want to, just show me where his bedroom is, and I will."

I'm not usually that aggressive, but the Spirit was moving me. In a little while—I think he took all the time he could—out came this inactive Aaronic Priesthood holder, ready for church.

That was the beginning of a great relationship between a boy and his priesthood advisor. This boy was a loner. He didn't have any friends in the ward—or anywhere else, for that matter. His only friend was his Jeep. But after that perilous Jeep ride, he and I did some other things together, and we grew to be friends. He became one of our most dependable priests and eventually served a full-time mission—not because of me or any special ability or talents I had but because a priest quorum advisor took his

Church calling seriously enough to ponder and pray and act on inspiration received.

Service Is Part of God's Plan

God the Father and Jesus Christ His Son have every right to expect much from you and me in service in the kingdom. According to the great plan of salvation, we all—by our own choice and agency—elected to follow the Lord rather than Lucifer. As a consequence of this choice, we earned the right to receive a physical body of flesh and bones. The blessing of receiving our mortal body perhaps will not be fully understood until we pass from this life into the next one.

Elder Melvin J. Ballard taught that concept this way: "We will never appreciate the value of this mortal body until we lose it. But when we do lose it, we will discover that we are entities just as real as we are here and now. We will look upon the house in which we have lived, this mortal tabernacle, as our friends do, discovering that we have eyes to see, that we have limbs and a body that to us is as real as the body we dwelt in while in mortality.

"We will be so real that it will take some of us days to convince ourselves we are dead, when we have separated from the body; and not until we turn to do what we used to do while in the body, and cannot do it, will it dawn upon us that we are dead, or that we are separated from the body" (*Sermons and Missionary Services,* 180). And then we will look forward in great anticipation to the day of resurrection when the body and the spirit can be reunited once again, never to be parted.

Receiving a physical body is absolutely essential if we are to achieve our goal to "dwell in the presence of God and his Christ forever and ever" (D&C 76:62). During the course of our mortal life, we can experience the testing process through exercising our moral agency. The God-given right to make our own choices is a fundamental part of our preparation for celestial living in the presence of God. Through this process we learn to either love and embrace the teachings and commandments of the gospel of Jesus Christ or to follow the temptations and enticements of the devil. Every human soul makes hundreds of choices daily; and when these are compounded and totaled, they will determine our eternal destiny. Never forget that one of life's most important choices is to repent and turn away from evil in order to embrace gospel standards. This process is part of the great plan of life. In our case, as members of the true Church of Jesus Christ, we have the perfect standard, or guideline, for knowing how to choose the right way to live in mortality. The gospel of Jesus Christ, with its teachings and commandments leading to eternal life, is what we must choose to follow. We are blessed while living in mortality to have both our physical body and spirit joined together. In this state of our existence, we are on the road to becoming like our Father in Heaven. As He Himself said after the fall of Adam, "Behold, the man has become as one of us, to know good and evil" (Genesis 3:22).

The prophet Alma explained the great experience of mortality as a probationary state or existence: "And we see that death comes upon mankind, yea, the death which has been spoken of by Amulek, which is the temporal death; nevertheless there was a space granted unto man in which he might repent; therefore this life became a probationary state; a time to prepare to meet God; a time to prepare for that endless state which has been spoken of by us, which is after the resurrection of the dead" (Alma 12:24).

And so, we are here in mortality with the physical body and the spirit united to help us work out our own salvation. The spirit within each us must learn to bring our body under subjection. By the power of our spirit, we must choose to embrace the commandments and teachings of the gospel of Jesus Christ. We are here to prove that we are trustworthy stewards of all that our Heavenly Father and the Lord Jesus Christ would entrust to our care. We demonstrate every day that we are learning to choose the right and to depart from evil. Through this process we are preparing to meet and live with God.

CALLED THROUGH REVELATION

The power of revelation from God to man is the way the Lord reveals His will to His servants. The process of extending calls to members to serve in the Church is a process of revelation. If you are true and faithful, if you repent and turn away from sin, revelation will come to your Church leaders at the ward, stake, and general levels to call you to serve in the callings that you have prepared yourself to receive as a result of exercising your agency in choosing to keep the commandments of the Lord.

Early in my ministry as a General Authority, I was sent by the Brethren to South America to divide a stake and choose new leadership for the new stake. Now, this may not sound like a very difficult assignment, but let me assure you that it is an important—and challenging—task. I knew the Lord had already chosen, by the process we have been discussing, the man he wanted for stake president. My job was to seek to know the mind and will of the Lord in order to extend on His behalf the call to serve. It is an overwhelming responsibility.

When I arrived at the stake to begin interviewing potential leaders, the current stake president told me that there were only three men who could possibly serve as stake president. Through an interpreter I explained to the stake president that the procedure of the Church was that I would interview all of the priesthood leaders living within the new stake.

Since there were more than thirty priesthood leaders to be interviewed through the interpreter, that process took considerably longer than usual. By late Saturday night, I had not yet found the person the Lord wanted to preside over this new stake. I reviewed once more with the stake president all of the potential leaders. We discovered that there was one man who lived in a small district that was being incorporated into the new stake. I learned that the reason he had not come in for an interview was that he was at home caring for his wife and three children, who were ill. Since telephone communication was limited in that part of South America, we had to send someone out to this brother's home, which was some distance away from where we were, to invite him to meet with me early Sunday morning.

When this fine man arrived, and I interviewed him, I knew he was the one the Lord had chosen to be the new stake president. Through thirty-four years of living he had been preparing for this call—by repenting of his sins and striving to keep the commandments of the gospel of Jesus Christ, by serving a full-time mission, by accepting responsibilities and leadership and teaching positions. The Prophet Joseph Smith taught that "every man who has a calling to minister to the inhabitants of the world was ordained to that very purpose in the Grand Council of heaven before this world was" (*Teachings of the Prophet Joseph Smith,* 365). It behooves every one of us to live as close to the teachings of the gospel as we can so we will not forfeit our foreordained opportunities to serve the Lord.

I called this faithful brother to serve at 7:20 A.M., knowing that the general session of the conference would begin in less than three hours' time. I couldn't see how he would ever select his counselors, organize his high council, and make other calls to leadership in such a short period of time. Expressing my concern that we were under such a terrible time constraint, this wonderful man smiled, reached into his shirt pocket, pulled out a piece of paper and then said to me, "Brother Ballard, I am prepared. I was told by the Spirit last night that I would be called to be the stake president. Here are my counselors, here are my high councilors, here are the others to serve as leaders of the stake."

The new stake was organized and the leaders sustained during the 10 A.M. session. Immediately following the general session, I set apart the leadership of the new stake. All was done through the use of interpreters and was possible only because revelation directed the callings of Heavenly Father's children.

SERVICE IN THE FAMILY

While service in the world and service in the Church are both important to the scriptural admonition to serve God by serving our fellow beings, there are no more important fellow beings for us to serve than those who live within the walls of our own homes. The Proclamation on the Family states that "husband and wife have a solemn responsibility to love and care for each other and for their children. 'Children are an heritage of the Lord' (Psalm 127:3). Parents have a sacred duty to rear their children in love and righteousness, to provide for their physical and spiritual needs, to teach them to love and serve one another, to observe the commandments of God and to be law-abiding citizens wherever they live. Husbands and wives—mothers and fathers—will be held accountable before God for the discharge of these obligations" (*Ensign,* November 1995, 102).

These are sacred duties—for spouses to "love and care for each other and for their children" and to teach their children to "love and serve one another." Can you imagine how much sweeter, how much happier, how much more wonderful the world would be if that one simple admonition was followed? There would be more love in the world and less litigation, more harmony and less discord, more cooperation and less friction, more peace and less abuse. Home would be a haven on earth, and the gospel message that "families can be together forever" would be viewed as more of a promise and less of a threat.

As parents we can begin to make this happen by using the same powerful technique that the Savior used with His disciples in teaching the same concept: that of example. Parents, teach your children to serve one another by serving them. You will find no sweeter satisfaction, no greater joy, no deeper fulfillment in your life than you will find in tender acts of service to the spirit children of God whom He has entrusted to you.

Shortly after we arrived in Toronto after being called to preside over the mission there, we were preparing the children to enroll in their new schools. My five-year-old son was to start kindergarten, but on the first day he was afraid to go. Barbara and I were concerned. Then I was impressed to invite my son to come into my office to sit in what the missionaries called the hot seat, and we would have an interview.

He climbed up into the big black chair, and I asked, "Son, how can I help you?"

I shall never forget as long as I live the look of real concern on his face. With his little chin quivering, he said, "Daddy, I am afraid."

I understood, for I knew he had left behind several friends of his same age, and so far he had found no one his age near the mission home. I said, "Craig, you have a friend who will always be with you. Let's kneel down together and ask Him to help you." We knelt, and Craig assigned me to say the prayer. The Lord helped Craig find his courage in this experience. Each morning for the next little while we held our interview, and every morning I was assigned to pray.

Then one morning there came no knock at my office door, no special father-and-son prayer. Craig had found his confidence and made some friends, and I was the one who missed that very special experience each morning with my little boy. This choice learning experience while in the mission field has remained with Craig and me and has been a source of strength to him in his own call to serve the Lord as a missionary, as a bishop, and in other Church callings.

The same is true in our ministry to our lovely daughters. We can serve these wonderful young women in unique and powerful ways that will teach gospel principles while confirming our love forever on their hearts and souls.

One of our daughters spent the full three years of high school in Canadian schools. When she was a senior, she came to me with this declaration: "Daddy, I have been studying for about thirty-five hours for a test in chemistry tomorrow, and I just simply do not understand. I have done everything I know how to do, and I am still confused. This material is vague in my mind. I know that when I sit down to take that test tomorrow that I am going to fail it. Can you help me?"

"Well, sweetheart," I said, "let me tell you about your dad and chemistry." I told her about the time my chemistry lab partner and I were working together in the East High School lab. We followed the instructions precisely—or so we thought. After mixing all the ingredients together, at the appropriate time we applied a match to our test tube, just as we had been told to do—except that while all the other test tubes in the lab burned appropriately, ours exploded. The bottom end of the tube shot across the laboratory into the wall. I can still see our teacher running toward us with his hands in the air, shouting, "Boys, boys, what have you done?'"

I looked at my seventeen-year-old daughter and said, "Sweetheart, to this day, I don't know what we did wrong. And you expect me to be able to help you with chemistry? We are in real trouble."

Then I made this proposal to her: "The only thing I know that I can do in the time that you have left is this. Let's go into the office and kneel down and ask the Lord, who knows all things, to bless you. Would you like that?" I was honored that she would ask for my help.

We slipped quietly into the office. What a thrill it was to kneel with my daughter and supplicate a special blessing from Heavenly Father, who loves her every bit as much as I do. And so we called upon Heavenly Father. We acknowledged Him as the Great Chemist. We acknowledged that He knew the beginning from the end. We did not ask for a miracle; we simply asked that He enlighten her mind and that somehow by the power of the Holy Ghost, bring back to her remembrance what she had studied for so long.

As we rose to our feet, she threw her arms around my neck and gave me a kiss. We stood there with tears in our eyes and knew that we were having a very special father-and-daughter experience.

She went off to school the next day with a degree of confidence. Two or three days later, she called me at the mission office and said, "Dad, guess what?" I could tell by the inflection in her voice that she had passed, but I wanted her to tell me.

"What, honey?" I asked.

"I passed the test!" she declared. "And that's not all. I got a good grade!"

I congratulated her for her accomplishment, but she had a hard time accepting much praise. "Dad," she said, "I don't know any more about chemistry now than I did before I took the test, but I passed!"

I was impressed at that moment to teach this principle: "Sweetheart, you might not know any more about chemistry, but you know a lot more about your Heavenly Father."

Such teaching moments come only to parents who are willing to invest time in meaningful service to their children. As with all kinds of service—including humanitarian service in the world, sharing the gospel, and fulfilling our Church callings— service in the home takes time and energy and requires a significant level of personal commitment. It may take you away from that ball game, or that business meeting, or the newspaper, or that household chore you've been putting off, but it will be infinitely worthwhile. Reaching out to others in unselfish service becomes a strong and secure link, especially when considered from within the context of the words of "A Poor Wayfaring Man of Grief":

> These deeds shall thy memorial be;
> Fear not, thou didst them unto me.

CHAPTER 8

HONORING THE PRIESTHOOD

Not long ago, two of our young missionaries were summoned to a California hospital to give a blessing to a young Latter-day Saint man who had been in a serious motorcycle accident. The nurse who called them was a member of the ward in which they were laboring, and she asked them to come as quickly as possible because the young man's condition was extremely critical.

When they arrived at the hospital, she apologized for having brought them there for nothing. The young man's condition had worsened. Scans revealed no brain activity. Monitors hooked to his body indicated that his various body systems were shutting down. Death was probably only minutes away.

The missionaries wondered if they should turn their ministerial attention to the young man's family. They were told that the highway patrol had contacted his parents in Utah, and they were making arrangements to come as quickly as possible. Still, they were at best hours away, and it appeared unlikely that they would arrive before their son died.

What a tragic situation. The missionaries asked if there was anything at all they could do to help. The nurse assured them that nothing could be done for the young man and suggested that perhaps they could return to provide comfort and support to his parents when they arrived. The missionaries said they would do so and turned to leave.

They had gone just a few steps down the hall, however, when an overwhelming feeling came to one of them. "If that were my son in that emergency room," he said to his companion, "I'd give him a blessing, no matter what the doctors said."

His companion agreed, and they quickly returned to the nurse.

"I appreciate what you're saying, elders," she said when they explained that they wanted to give the young man a priesthood blessing. "But he's dying. He may already be dead. There's nothing anyone can do about that."

The missionaries looked at each other for a moment. Then one of them spoke. "You're right—there's nothing I can do about it," he said. "But the blessing won't come from me. It will come from God. Why don't we see what He has to say in the matter?"

The nurse led them to the young man's bedside, where one of them anointed his heavily bandaged head with consecrated oil. The other missionary joined his companion in placing their hands delicately on the patient's head, careful to avoid all of the tubes and wires that were keeping the young man barely alive. The anointing was sealed, and the missionary who was acting as voice waited for the Spirit to prompt the words of the blessing. He was not impressed to give a blessing of healing or recovery; rather, he was prompted to bless the young man that he would live long enough to see and speak to his parents when they arrived.

That is precisely what happened, much to the amazement of the entire medical staff of the hospital. For several hours, the young man hovered precariously between life and death. But he rallied significantly when his parents arrived. He even regained consciousness long enough to speak to them briefly before he died.

The missionaries returned to the hospital to speak to this young man's parents, from whom they learned the rest of the story. Their son had been estranged from them and from the Church for several years but had recently made some important changes in his life, including a return to activity in the Church. He was on his way home to Utah for a reconciliation with his family when the accident occurred. During the brief time he regained consciousness, he was able to express his love to his parents, and they were able to express their love to him. It was a healing time for the entire family—spiritually, if not physically.

When the parents thanked the emergency room staff for their care of their son, one of the doctors rejected their suggestion that the skill of the medical personnel had something to do with the young man's staying alive as long as he did. "It's nothing that we did," the doctor said. "I don't even know how he was able to regain consciousness to communicate with you. I'm not sure I believe in miracles, but there's no other explanation for what happened here today."

Ever since the priesthood of God was restored to the earth through the Prophet Joseph Smith, miraculous things have happened in the lives of Latter-day Saints. In addition to miracles of healing, priesthood power is manifest almost daily throughout the Church through miracles of revelation, miracles of service, miracles of organization, and miracles of administration. Under the direction of latter-day prophets and Apostles, priesthood authority is exercised in behalf of Heavenly Father's children, and priesthood keys are used to unlock the mysteries of His kingdom.

Priesthood authority has certainly not been limited to this dispensation. Said the Prophet Joseph Smith: "The priesthood is an everlasting principle, and existed with God from eternity, and will to eternity, without beginning of days or end of years"

(*Teachings of the Prophet Joseph Smith,* 157; see also 158, 323). Adam held the priesthood (Moses 6:67-68), as did other Old Testament and Book of Mormon prophets (*Teachings of the Prophet Joseph Smith,* 181). Moses, for example, used priesthood power to work miracles in the court of Pharaoh and to part the Red Sea.

The Savior's mortal ministry was an age of miracles, wrought through the authority and power of His holy priesthood. He healed the sick, cast out devils, gave sight to the blind, and raised the dead. This same priesthood was given to His Apostles so that they would have "power and authority over all devils, and to cure diseases. And he sent them to preach the kingdom of God, and to heal the sick" (Luke 9:1-2).

When the priesthood was restored to the earth to usher in the dispensation of the fulness of times, it was returned with miracles intact. Joseph Smith, Brigham Young, John Taylor, and other early Church leaders had extraordinary experiences as they began to understand the power of their priesthood authority. According to President Taylor, priesthood "is the government of God, whether on the earth or in the heavens, for it is by that power, agency, or principle that all things are governed on the earth and in the heavens, and by that power that all things are upheld and sustained. It governs all things—it directs all things, it sustains all things—and has to do with all things that God and truth are associated with" (*Millennial Star* 9 [1 November 1847]: 321).

I testify that the priesthood of God is upon the earth today and that through it miraculous things are happening in the lives of our members and others all around the world. Respecting and honoring that priesthood, therefore, is another one of the links in our chain which brings happiness and success in this life—and the next.

"WALKING IN DARKNESS AT NOON-DAY"

Unfortunately, not all of us appreciate what it means to have such direct access to priesthood authority. I am especially concerned that some of our brethren who hold the priesthood are severely limited in their understanding of the great power and authority that is theirs.

In that way we haven't come all that far from the days of Joseph Smith, when the Lord pointed out that "there are many who have been ordained among you, whom I have called but few of them are chosen. They who are not chosen have sinned a very grievous sin, in that they are walking in darkness at noon-day" (D&C 95:5-6).

To possess priesthood authority without fully appreciating and exercising its potential power for righteous influence in our own lives, in our homes and families, and in the world around us is like "walking in darkness at noon-day." That is why so many who have been called to receive the priesthood have not been chosen to experience the sweet fulfillment that comes when "the doctrine of the priesthood [distills] upon thy soul as the dews from heaven" (D&C 121:45).

"And why are they not chosen?" the Lord asks in Doctrine and Covenants 121. And then he provides an interesting answer to his own question:

"Because their hearts are set so much upon the things of this world, and aspire to the honors of men, that they do not learn this one lesson—that the rights of the priesthood are inseparably connected with the powers of heaven, and that the powers of heaven cannot be controlled nor handled only upon the principles of righteousness. That they may be conferred upon us, it is true; but when we undertake to cover our sins, or to gratify our pride, our vain ambition, or to exercise control or dominion or compulsion upon the souls of the children of men, in any degree of unrighteousness, behold, the heavens withdraw themselves; the Spirit of the Lord is grieved; and when it is withdrawn, Amen to the priesthood or the authority of that man" (D&C 121:34-37).

It seems to me that the Lord is suggesting that if we are not experiencing the miracles of priesthood power in our own lives, perhaps we have not sufficiently developed those "principles of righteousness." Later in the same section, the Lord identifies some of those principles: "persuasion . . . long-suffering . . . gentleness and meekness . . . love unfeigned . . . kindness, and pure knowledge . . . charity . . . faith . . . virtue" (D&C 121:41-45).

To those who do cultivate these wonderful characteristics, the Lord promises that "thy confidence [shall] wax strong in the presence of God; and the doctrine of the priesthood shall distil upon thy soul as the dews from heaven. The Holy Ghost shall be thy constant companion, and thy scepter an unchanging scepter of righteousness and truth; and thy dominion shall be an everlasting dominion, and without compulsory means it shall flow unto thee forever and ever" (D&C 121:45-46).

Great and marvelous are the blessings the Lord promises to those who righteously honor and exercise His priesthood authority. Conversely, those who receive the priesthood and choose not to follow the principles of righteousness are left unto themselves to "kick against the pricks, to persecute the saints, and to fight against God" (D&C 121:38). It is well for us to do everything in our power to be both called and chosen by honoring and responding to priesthood authority.

MAGNIFYING THE PRIESTHOOD

It isn't enough to receive the priesthood righteously, however. According to the Lord's instruction to Joseph Smith in Doctrine and Covenants 84, miraculous blessings await those who are "faithful unto the obtaining [of the priesthood], . . . and the magnifying their calling": They "are sanctified by the Spirit unto the renewing of their bodies. All they who receive this priesthood receive me, saith the Lord; for he that receiveth my servants receiveth me; and he that receiveth me receiveth my Father; and he that receiveth my Father receiveth my Father's kingdom; therefore all that my Father hath shall be given unto him" (D&C 84:33, 35–38).

Think about that for a moment: "All that my Father hath shall be given unto him." There is no greater miracle than that. But this miracle isn't available to all priesthood holders. According to the revelation often referred to as the oath and covenant of the priesthood, it is reserved for those who faithfully receive the priesthood and who magnify their priesthood callings.

What does it mean to magnify a priesthood calling? I believe it means precisely what the word *magnify* suggests. It means to become enlarged in our calling. It means to take our priesthood calling—whatever that calling is—and make it more important, more meaningful, more significant, more valuable because of the way we apply ourselves to it. There is no such thing as "just an elder," "just a home teacher," or "just a Primary worker" to the priesthood holder who magnifies his calling. Every calling is gratefully accepted, prayerfully prepared, and joyfully executed. It is valued. Enlarged. Magnified.

Those who magnify their priesthood office also understand that their most important work is performed within the walls of their own homes. They are faithful husbands, devoted fathers, and loyal sons. They lead out in family prayer, family scripture study, and family home evening. They honor, respect, and cherish the women in their lives. When they are called upon to give priesthood blessings, they do so confidently and worthily.

During the April 1957 general conference of the Church, Elder Delbert L. Stapley of the Council of the Twelve Apostles asked this telling question: "Can a man magnify his calling who is not willing to sacrifice and consecrate all for the building of God's kingdom in righteousness, truth, and power in the earth?" (Conference Report, April 1957, 77).

I testify that he cannot. Even though men have the rights of the priesthood conferred upon them, they cannot reap its eternal blessings if they exercise their priesthood authority unrighteously or unworthily. Nor can they experience the miraculous manifestations of priesthood power historically associated with God's authority on the earth if they are not spiritually prepared to do so.

PRIESTHOOD IS FOR SERVICE

Priesthood offices are not status symbols but opportunities for service. High priests, elders, priests, teachers, and deacons are equally responsible to serve faithfully in the offices to which they have been called. All priesthood holders assist our Heavenly Father in accomplishing His divine purpose: "to bring to pass the immortality and eternal life of man" (Moses 1:39).

Consider these words of the sixth President of the Church, Joseph F. Smith: "There is no office growing out of this Priesthood that is or can be greater than the Priesthood itself. It is from the Priesthood that the office derives its authority and power. No office gives authority to the Priesthood. No office adds to the power of the Priesthood" (*Gospel Doctrine,* 148).

The priesthood itself cannot be magnified nor diminished, but one who worthily uses his priesthood in service to others can magnify his calling in the priesthood.

All who hold the priesthood of God are joined together in a common bond of service. The resurrected John the Baptist expressed this concept on that sacred occasion when he restored the Aaronic Priesthood to men on earth. This angelic messenger from God, the same who had been privileged to baptize the Savior, addressed the Prophet Joseph Smith and his associate in the work, Oliver Cowdery, as "my fellow servants" (D&C 13:1). What a marvelous model for humble service in the kingdom of God!

Each man or boy who holds the priesthood, regardless of his priesthood or his ordained office, is a fellow servant in the work of the Lord Jesus Christ. Although I have been ordained to the office of Apostle in the Melchizedek Priesthood, I and my associates in that office are fellow servants in the work of the Lord with the most recently ordained deacon or elder in the Church. Although the Apostle Paul stated the truth that "God hath set . . . first apostles [in the Church]," he also stated the truth that each member of the body is necessary. No one in any priesthood office can say of those in other offices, "I have no need of thee," because we all are fellow servants in the service of the Lord (1 Corinthians 12:14–28). Our common and most important objective is to do His work.

Each priesthood bearer, acting within the duties of his calling, is needed to accomplish the work of the Lord. I repeat, a priesthood office is bestowed not for status but for service. All priesthood bearers are fellow servants in the Church of Jesus Christ.

In addition to holding an ordained office in the priesthood, most priesthood bearers also are called to a specific position in their ward or stake. For example, a brother holding the priesthood may be called to serve in a quorum presidency, as a teacher in a Sunday School or Primary class, as a member of a ward or quorum committee, or as a stake officer. In each of these callings, he serves for a time and then is released to give another an opportunity to serve where he has labored. He then will receive other opportunities to serve. Callings may change, but the need for constant and committed service in some capacity will continue. The responsibility to honor and magnify the priesthood is an eternal obligation.

As we serve together, we must serve in humility, always being kind and considerate of one another. A few years ago, I reorganized the Belfast Ireland Stake. Raymond Lowry was called to be the new stake president. At the time of his call, he was serving as second counselor to Bishop Bowyer. President Lowry selected Bishop Bowyer to serve as his first counselor in the newly organized stake presidency. Can you see why we should always be kind to one another? We never know in this Church who will be presiding over us tomorrow.

I recall the story told by Elder Boyd K. Packer of a stake president in England who had served with great effectiveness over a period of years. When the time came for his release, this humble leader said: "I was happy to accept the call to serve as stake president, and I am equally happy to accept my release. I did not serve just because I was under call. I served because I am under covenant. And I can keep my covenants quite as well as a home teacher as I can serving as stake president" (in Boyd K. Packer, *Ensign*, May 1987, 24).

Recently, I asked a wonderful priesthood bearer, ninety-five years old and serving as a temple worker, to join in the circle when I set his son apart to serve as stake president. I commended the father for his lifelong faithful service, and he responded, "Brother Ballard, you do not pray for your leaders all of your life and then turn them down when they call you to do something." This is the true spirit of being a servant in the kingdom of God.

Occasionally, we hear that some of our older brethren, feeling perhaps that they have done their duty, think they have reached a stage of retirement from active service in the Church. You may have heard the story about one high priest who passed out during priesthood meeting. Thinking the man had suffered a heart attack, his group leader called the paramedics. According to the story, they carried out five sleeping high priests before they found the one who had passed out. We may find some humor in this story, but I trust the message is not lost. Let us never be asleep at our posts. No office in the priesthood is given as a sedative; rather, it is a stimulant for service.

Shortly after returning from my first mission, I heard our faithful stake patriarch bear his testimony in our ward fast and testimony meeting. He was just over ninety years of age; he said, "I pray every night that God will see me safely dead with my testimony burning brightly." Seeking to comfort this righteous patriarch, I said to him, "Patriarch, I know of no one more prepared than you are." He responded, "My boy, no one is safe until he has endured to the very end of his life."

Brethren, regardless of your priesthood office or your years of membership and service in the Church, you always can do more. To receive the priesthood is to make an eternal commitment to serving others.

President David O. McKay declared: "Priesthood means service. This is true even in its divine source, as we may infer from the sublime declaration: 'This is my work and my glory—to bring to pass the immortality and eternal life of man.' Emanating from Deity is the service that leads to the redemption of God's children" (*Pathways to Happiness,* 231).

Similarly, please consider the words of President Marion G. Romney: "Service is not something we endure on this earth so we can earn the right to live in the celestial kingdom. Service is the very fiber of which an exalted life in the celestial kingdom is made.

"Knowing that service is what gives our Father in Heaven fulfillment, and knowing that we want to be where He is and as He is, why must we be commanded to serve one another? . . . Service is what Godhood is all about" (*Ensign,* November 1982, 93).

STAND FOR TRUTH AND RIGHT

Priesthood holders have a sacred duty always to stand for truth and right. The priesthood, by definition, is God's authority given to man to do the things that He would do if He were here. That means not only are we His witnesses but we are His representatives.

As a Church we recognize that the gospel of Jesus Christ,

with its saving truths and teachings, provides the most effective preventative and rehabilitative assistance in overcoming sinful behavior. The most effective power against adversarial evil is priesthood power. Parents bear the first and greatest responsibility to teach their children principles of gospel living and good citizenship, but priesthood quorums and leaders need to be aware of those who have little or no support at home and do all they can to bless their lives. Such individuals will be blessed in having positive role models who demonstrate integrity by honoring their covenants and keeping their promises.

What a great blessing it is to bear and to honor the priesthood of God. This sacred power is surely a link in our chain that needs to be kept strong and pure if faith is to remain a firm anchor in our lives and in the lives of those whom we serve.

CHAPTER 9

HONORING WOMANHOOD

Some time ago I received the following outline, called "A Woman's Lifeline." Perhaps you will see in it a reflection of yourself or someone you love.

Age 3:   She looks at herself and sees a Queen.

Age 8:   She looks at herself and sees Cinderella.

Age 15:   She looks at herself and sees an Ugly Duck-ling. ("Mom, I can't go to school looking like this!")

Age 20:   She looks at herself and sees "too fat/too thin, too short/too tall, too straight/too curly"—but decides she's going out anyway.

Age 30:   She looks at herself and sees "too fat/too thin, too short/too tall, too straight/too curly"—but decides she doesn't have time to fix it so she's going out anyway.

Age 40:   She looks at herself and sees "too fat/too thin, too short/too tall, too straight/too curly"—but says, "At least I am clean," and goes out anyway.

Age 50:   She looks at herself and sees "I am what I
            am" and goes wherever she wants to go.
Age 60:   She looks at herself and reminds herself of
            all the people who can't even see themselves
            in the mirror anymore. Goes out and con-
            quers the world.
Age 70:   She looks at herself and sees wisdom, laugh-
            ter, and ability. Goes out and enjoys life.
Age 80:   Doesn't bother to look. Just puts on a purple
            hat and goes out to have fun with the world.

Maybe we should all grab that purple hat earlier.

Maybe we should! It is my hope that every member of the
Church—male and female—would recognize the intrinsic value
women have as daughters of a loving Heavenly Father. As we
continue throughout our lives to forge the links in our chain, we
must not overlook that of honoring womanhood. To honor
womanhood is to deemphasize the worldly considerations of
"too fat/too thin, too short/too tall, too straight/too curly." Let
us ever remember the wisdom of Proverbs: "Who can find a virtuous woman? for her price is far above rubies. . . . Strength and
honour are her clothing . . . and in her tongue is the law of kindness" (Proverbs 31:10, 25-26).

Can any of us reflect on the scene surrounding the birth of
our Savior and not marvel at the inner "strength and honour"
of Mary, that "precious and chosen vessel" who bore the Christ
child? (Alma 7:10).

Sometime during the festivities celebrating the birth of the
Christ child, I begin to wonder what must have been in Mary's
mind as she held the Baby in her arms—the awesome wonder-
ment of what had happened to her, the declaration of the
angels, the proclamation that she would conceive by the Father,
that she would bear a son, that His name would be Jesus, that

He would be the Son of God, the Savior and the Redeemer of the world.

After hearing all of the things she heard and witnessing so many marvelous things, I suppose Mary still went through the natural, normal processes of rearing her child. We read in the scriptures that "the child grew, and waxed strong in spirit, filled with wisdom: and the grace of God was upon him" (Luke 2:40).

Her son matured to the age of twelve, and we learn of this experience: "Now his parents went to Jerusalem every year at the feast of the passover.

"And when he was twelve years old, they went up to Jerusalem after the custom of the feast.

"And when they had fulfilled the days, as they returned, the child Jesus tarried behind in Jerusalem; and Joseph and his mother knew not [of it].

"But they, supposing him to have been in the company, went a day's journey; and they sought him among [their] kinsfolk and acquaintance.

"And when they found him not, they turned back again to Jerusalem, seeking him.

"And it came to pass, that after three days they found him in the temple, sitting in the midst of the doctors, both hearing them, and asking them questions.

"And all that heard him were astonished at his understanding and answers.

"And when they saw him, they were amazed: and his mother said unto him, Son, why hast thou thus dealt with us? behold, thy father and I have sought thee sorrowing.

"And he said unto them, How is it that ye sought me? wist ye not that I must be about my Father's business?" (Luke 2:41–49).

I think about the profound effect that must have had on Mary—her twelve-year-old Son sitting in the temple, teaching the learned men of His day, answering their questions, and then reminding her of His true sireship. This short verse follows that experience: "His mother kept all these sayings in her heart" (Luke 2:51).

I have great affection for the mother of Jesus. His relationship with her gives us a sense of His respect for her and for all women. As in all things, the Savior sets the perfect example for all of us in how we should relate to our mothers, to our sisters, and to all the women of the Church. Elder James E. Talmage stated: "The world's greatest champion of woman and womanhood is Jesus Christ" (*Jesus the Christ*, 475).

Three scriptural examples from His life should make that point abundantly clear.

CHRIST AND THE WOMAN AT THE WELL

"Then cometh he to a city of Samaria. . . . [Please keep in mind that He is in His ministry here, going about doing good and teaching the gospel.]

"Now Jacob's well was there. Jesus therefore, being wearied with his journey, sat thus on the well: and it was about the sixth hour.

"There cometh a woman of Samaria to draw water: Jesus saith unto her, Give me to drink. . . .

"Then saith the woman of Samaria unto him, How is it that thou, being a Jew, askest drink of me, which am a woman of Samaria? for the Jews have no dealings with the Samaritans.

"Jesus answered and said unto her, If thou knewest the gift of God, and who it is that saith to thee, Give me to drink; thou wouldest have asked of him, and he would have given thee living water.

"The woman saith unto him, Sir, thou hast nothing to draw with, and the well is deep: from whence then hast thou that living water?

"Art thou greater than our father Jacob, which gave us the

well, and drank thereof himself, and his children, and his cattle?

"Jesus answered and said unto her, Whosoever drinketh of this water shall thirst again:

"But whosoever drinketh of the water that I shall give him shall never thirst; but the water that I shall give him shall be in him a well of water springing up into everlasting life" (John 4:5-14).

You remember the dialogue that took place between Jesus and the woman at the well. She said that she didn't have a husband, and He reminded her that she had had five husbands. Then the dialogue continues:

"Ye worship ye know not what: we know what we worship: for salvation is of the Jews.

"But the hour cometh, and now is, when the true worshippers shall worship the Father in spirit and in truth: for the Father seeketh such to worship him. . . .

"The woman saith unto him, I know that Messias cometh, which is called Christ: when he is come, he will tell us all things.

"Jesus saith unto her, I that speak unto thee am he" (John 4:22-26).

That is the first declaration we have in recorded scripture of the Savior of the world testifying and witnessing to someone else—a woman of Samaria—that He was the Messiah, the Son of God. Clearly, the Lord did not consider it beneath His dignity to share so significant a message with her.

"The woman then left her water pot, and went her way into the city, and saith to the men,

"Come, see a man, which told me all things that ever I did: is not this the Christ?

"Then they went out of the city, and came unto him" (John 4:28-30).

"And many of the Samaritans of that city believed on him for the saying of the woman, which testified, He told me all that ever I did.

"So when the Samaritans were come unto him, they besought him that he would tarry with them: and he abode there two days.

"And many more believed because of his own word;

"And said unto the woman, Now we believe, not because of thy saying: for we have heard him ourselves, and know that this is indeed the Christ, the Saviour of the world" (John 4:39–42).

MARY AND MARTHA

We all know of the affection that the Savior had for Mary and Martha and Lazarus. I have a sense that for Jesus, visiting Bethany was like coming home because He had no home of His own. My study of the scriptures leads me to believe that this family was special to the Savior, and wonderful were the teachings that He gave to Mary and Martha. Of course, none were greater than the magnificent manifestation of His divine authority that followed the death of Lazarus. You will remember that Jesus was out of town when Lazarus died. As soon as she heard Jesus had returned, Martha ran to meet Him, to share with Him the sad news. She expressed complete faith that had Jesus been there, He could have saved her brother's life.

"Jesus saith unto her, Thy brother shall rise again.

"Martha saith unto him, I know that he shall rise again in the resurrection at the last day.

"Jesus said unto her, I am the resurrection, and the life: he that believeth in me, though he were dead, yet shall he live:

"And whosoever liveth and believeth in me shall never die. Believest thou this?

"She saith unto him, Yea, Lord: I believe that thou art the Christ, the Son of God, which should come into the world" (John 11:23–27).

Mary joined them, and together they went to Lazarus's

tomb, where the Savior commanded the dead man to rise that Mary and Martha "shouldest see the glory of God" (John 11:40). Such was His love for them and respect and appreciation for their faith in Him.

BELIEVING HEARTS OF BELIEVING WOMEN

Believing hearts of believing women were an important part of the Savior's mortal ministry, right up until that awful day when He was raised up on the cross.

The scriptures record:

"Now there stood by the cross of Jesus his mother, and his mother's sister, Mary the wife of Cleophas, and Mary Magdalene.

"When Jesus therefore saw his mother, and the disciple standing by, whom he loved, he saith unto his mother, Woman, behold thy son!

"Then saith he to the disciple, Behold thy mother! And from that hour that disciple took her unto his own home" (John 19:25-27).

There are not words—certainly I don't have them—capable of expressing the feelings in the heart of Jesus' mother as she, I suppose, knelt at the base of the cross witnessing the fulfillment of the divine proclamation that we sing of and herald at Christmas time, the story of the birth of the babe in Bethlehem. I can't help but wonder if Mary knew, even as she held her newborn Son in her arms in that lowly stable, that one day she would be here, at the foot of His cross, as He paid the final, awful price of His Messianic destiny.

My heart goes out in tribute to Mary the mother of Jesus and to all of the women who stood by Him in faith and hope and were there at His side to share His final moments in mortality. And I rejoice to know it was also a woman who was the first to see the resurrected Lord on Easter morning.

"The first day of the week cometh Mary Magdalene early,

when it was yet dark, unto the sepulchre, and seeth the stone taken away from the sepulchre.

"Then she runneth, and cometh to Simon Peter, and to the other disciple, whom Jesus loved, and saith unto them, They have taken away the Lord out of the sepulchre, and we know not where they have laid him" (John 20:1-2).

Remember, the disciples ran back with her to the sepulchre. They too witnessed that it was empty. I suppose they discussed the matter. Then the scriptures record that "the disciples went away again unto their own home" (John 20:10).

But not Mary.

"Mary stood without at the sepulchre weeping: and as she wept, she stooped down, and looked into the sepulchre,

"And seeth two angels in white sitting, the one at the head, and the other at the feet, where the body of Jesus had lain.

"And they say unto her, Woman, why weepest thou? She saith unto them, Because they have taken away my Lord, and I know not where they have laid him.

"And when she had thus said, she turned herself back, and saw Jesus standing, and knew not that it was Jesus.

"Jesus saith unto her, Woman, why weepest thou? whom seekest thou? She, supposing him to be the gardener, saith unto him, Sir, if thou have borne him hence, tell me where thou hast laid him, and I will take him away.

"Jesus saith unto her, Mary" (John 20:11-16).

I find it meaningful that the first uttered words of the first resurrected being, as it pertains to the creation of this world, were spoken to this wonderful, faithful, brokenhearted woman.

"She turned herself, and saith unto him, Rabboni; which is to say, Master.

"Jesus saith unto her, Touch me not; for I am not yet ascended to my Father: but go to my brethren, and say unto them, I ascend unto my Father, and your Father; and to my God, and your God.

"Mary Magdalene came and told the disciples that she had seen the Lord, and that he had spoken these things unto her" (John 20:16–18).

Again, it is significant to me that this message was carried to the disciples, the Apostles of the Lord Jesus Christ, by a woman, Mary Magdalene. I don't believe that was coincidental. The Savior's profound love and respect for the women in His life made the annunciation to Mary Magdalene completely natural and appropriate.

WOMEN OF FAITH AND COURAGE

Faithful women have labored valiantly in the cause of truth and righteousness from before the foundations of this world. They have always been vital and integral to the work of the Lord. In President Joseph F. Smith's vision of the redemption of the dead, he saw not only Father Adam and other prophets but "our glorious Mother Eve, with many of her faithful daughters who had lived through the ages and worshiped the true and living God" (D&C 138:39).

Mother Eve enjoyed with her husband, Adam, the beauties and wonders and peace of Eden. It was she who rejoiced in her understanding that "were it not for our transgression we never should have had seed, and never should have known good and evil, and the joy of our redemption, and the eternal life which God giveth unto all the obedient" (Moses 5:11).

An entire community of mothers changed the course of Book of Mormon history by virtue of their powerful influence upon their sons. During a time of extraordinary danger, the Nephite nation was preserved and protected by the valiant efforts of Helaman and his band of two thousand stripling warriors, the sons of the people of Ammon.

"And they were all young men, and they were exceedingly valiant for courage, and also for strength and activity; but behold, this was not all—they were men who were true at all times in whatsoever thing they were entrusted.

"Yea, they were men of truth and soberness, for they had been taught to keep the commandments of God and to walk uprightly before him" (Alma 53:20–21).

Speaking of these outstanding young men, Helaman wrote to tell his brother Moroni that "never had I seen so great courage, nay, not amongst all the Nephites" (Alma 56:45).

"Now they never had fought, yet they did not fear death; and they did think more upon the liberty of their fathers than they did upon their lives; yea, they had been taught by their mothers, that if they did not doubt, God would deliver them.

"And they rehearsed unto me the words of their mothers," Helaman continued, "saying: We do not doubt our mothers knew it" (Alma 56:47–48).

How marvelous is the extraordinary power for life-changing influence by faithful women!

In my own family history, I trace my spiritual and physical roots to extraordinary women of faith and courage. My great-great-grandmother was Mary Fielding Smith, the wife of Hyrum Smith, the patriarch. She was an eyewitness to many of the miraculous events of the Restoration, and she cultivated a deep and abiding testimony that saw her through the martyrdom of her husband and the hardships of moving her family across the plains to Utah. Two of her posterity—Joseph F. Smith and Joseph Fielding Smith—became Presidents of the Church; others became Apostles. Many have served as leaders in the wards and stakes of the Church. To this day, her influence for good is felt throughout the Church.

Looking back on his mother's influence on his life, President Joseph F. Smith said, "I am at a loss to know . . . how it would be possible for anyone to love her children more truly than did my mother. I have felt sometimes, how could even the Father love his children more than my mother loved her children? It was life to me; it was strength; it was encouragement; it was love that begat love or liking in myself. I knew she loved me with all her heart. She loved her children with all her soul. She would toil and labor and sacrifice herself day and night, for the temporal comforts and blessings that she could meagerly give, through the results of her own labors, to her children. There was no sacrifice of self—of her own time, of her leisure or pleasure, or opportunities for rest—that was considered for a moment, when it was compared with her duty and her love to her children.

"When I was fifteen years of age, and called to go to a foreign country to preach the gospel," President Smith continued, "the strongest anchor that was fixed in my life, and that helped to hold my ambition and my desire steady, to bring me upon a level and keep me straight, was that love which I knew she had for me who bore me into the world. Only a little boy, not matured at all in judgment, without the advantage of education, thrown in the midst of the greatest allurements and temptations that it was possible for any boy or any man to be subjected to—and yet, whenever these temptations became most alluring and most tempting to me, the first thought that arose in my soul was this: Remember the love of your mother. Remember how she strove for your welfare. Remember how willing she was to sacrifice her life for your good. Remember what she taught you in your childhood and how she insisted upon your reading the New Testament—the only book, except a few little school books, that we had in the family, or that was within reach of us at that time. This feeling toward my mother became a defense, a barrier between me and temptation, so that I could turn aside from temptation and sin by the help of the Lord and the love begotten in my soul, toward her whom I knew loved me more than anybody else in all the world, and more than any other living being could love me" (*Gospel Doctrine*, 314-15).

My Ballard line also has remarkable women exemplars. I

mention specifically one who was an early convert to the restored gospel: Margaret McNeil Ballard, my great-grandmother. She was born in Scotland in 1845, one year after her father joined the Church. Although they were eager to join the Saints in Utah, Church callings, including that of Margaret's father to be the branch president, kept them in Tranent for a time. They sailed for New York in 1856. After experiencing several more delays, eleven-year-old Margaret and her family finally began their journey west. From Margaret's personal history, we know that measles broke out, and all of her siblings became very sick. The rest of the company moved on without them. Because Margaret did not take sick, her mother was anxious for her to remain with the company. Margaret recorded: "My mother strapped my little brother James on my back with a shawl. He was only four years old and still quite sick with the measles, but I took him since mother had all she could do to care for the other children. I hurried and caught up with the company, traveling with them all day. That night a kind lady helped me take my brother off my back. I sat up and held him on my lap with the shawl wrapped around him, alone, all night. He was a little better in the morning. The people in the camp were very good to us and gave us a little fried bacon and some bread for breakfast.

"We traveled this way for about a week, my brother and I not seeing our mother during this time. Each morning one of the men would write a note and put it in the slit of a willow stuck into the ground to tell how we were getting along. In this way mother knew we were all right."

Margaret ends this part of her account with these words, "We arrived in Ogden on the fourth day of October, 1859, after a journey of hardships and hunger, with thankfulness to our Heavenly Father for his protecting care."

She had walked every step of the way across the plains and

for a large part of the way had carried her brother James on her back. Her feet were often wrapped only in bloodstained rags.

Once in the dark of night she was sent to retrieve their cow which had wandered away. She was barefoot and unable to see clearly where she was walking. Suddenly, she began to feel that she was walking on something soft. She stopped and looked down to see what it could be. She wrote: "To my horror I found that I was standing in a bed of snakes, large ones and small ones. At the sight of them I became so weak that I could scarcely move. All I could think of was to pray."

Margaret went on to serve faithfully as a ward Relief Society president for thirty years and by the side of her good husband, who was a bishop in Logan for thirty-nine years.

Each of these women exemplified great courage and steadfastness throughout their lives. Their indomitable will came from their faith, faith in God and in His Son, Jesus Christ.

Such women, now as then, wield a tremendous influence in the Church—and in the world.

THE POWER OF WOMANHOOD

If *power* seems to be an unusual choice of words to use in connection with the women of the Church, where we tend to associate power with priesthood, please be assured that the choice is quite intentional. I have the utmost respect, reverence, and appreciation for the power of the priesthood and its divine authority to perform the saving ordinances of the gospel, but I also understand that "the rights of the priesthood are inseparably connected with the powers of heaven, and that the powers of heaven cannot be controlled nor handled only upon the principles of righteousness" (D&C 121:36).

As in honoring the priesthood, those "principles of righteousness" through which one can control—or at least draw upon—the "powers of heaven" include such traits as "persuasion . . . long-suffering . . . gentleness . . . meekness . . . love unfeigned

... kindness, and pure knowledge, which shall greatly enlarge the soul without hypocrisy, and without guile" (D&C 121:41-42). As I consider these traits through which God empowers His people, certainly there is found a rich tradition of gentleness, meekness, love, and kindness among the women of the Church. And I am aware that there is much of persuasion, long-suffering, and pure knowledge and little of hypocrisy and guile among them as well.

Therefore when women cultivate these attributes they enjoy the power of their nature and are a great influence among all women—in fact among all people everywhere. That influence is real, and it is awesome. It is the power of faith. It is the power of purity. And it is the power of love, that which the Apostle Paul called charity, the greatest of all godly virtues (1 Corinthians 13:13).

Access to such wondrous and incredible power is available to Heavenly Father's daughters and sons through the plan that He Himself designed for the eternal welfare of His children. This plan originated long before any of us were born. It is God's plan. The doctrine is His, and His alone. It is not subject to mortal whim, expediency, or the ever-changing winds of political correctness.

As the Lord said through the prophet Isaiah: "For my thoughts are not your thoughts, neither are your ways my ways, saith the Lord. For as the heavens are higher than the earth, so are my ways higher than your ways, and my thoughts than your thoughts" (Isaiah 55:8-9).

For example, we don't know why God has chosen to give His priesthood authority to men and not to women. We know it is not because men are inherently more righteous or more faithful than women, because that simply is not true. Heavenly Father has only chosen to reveal His will on the matter, not His reasoning. Indeed, the reasons are unimportant as far as we are concerned because the issue is not open to debate. Consensus and public opinion are irrelevant to a discussion of the doctrine

of God because it is mandated through revelation, not legisla-
tion. For us, the only thing that matters is whether we choose
to accept the doctrine and abide by its precepts. It is an issue of
faith—nothing more, nothing less.

Sometimes our faith is tested. Many Relief Society presidents
are frustrated when they sit in council with priesthood leaders
who do not take their stewardship as seriously as they should
or who do not treat them with respect. Other women have been
dominated, manipulated, and, in some horrifying cases, cruelly
abused by men who wield their priesthood authority like a club
over the heads of women who trust them and who want to
honor and respect the priesthood.

At such times it is important to remember two simple truths.
First, you need to understand that men who use priesthood in
this manner have no authority to do so. The Lord told Joseph
Smith that "when we undertake to cover our sins, or to gratify
our pride, our vain ambition, or to exercise control or dominion or compulsion upon the souls of the children of men, in any
degree of unrighteousness, behold, the heavens withdraw themselves; the Spirit of the Lord is grieved; and when it is withdrawn, Amen to the priesthood or the authority of that man"
(D&C 121:37).

In other words, one who lays claim to special privilege
through priesthood does not understand the nature of his
authority. Priesthood is about service, not servitude; compassion, not compulsion; caring, not control; stewardship, not turf.
Those who would have you think otherwise are operating outside the parameters of their authority.

The second thing you should remember in this regard has
to do with the principle of moral agency. Heavenly Father feels
so strongly about protecting the precious gift of moral agency
that He will allow all of His children to exercise it—for good or
for evil. Of course, He has an eternal perspective that helps Him
to understand that whatever pain and suffering we endure in

this life—regardless of its origins and causes—it is only a moment compared with our entire eternal existence.

As mortals, however, we are rarely able to view life from that clear perspective. Instead, we feel pain and anguish in the face of adversity, for ourselves and for others. But faith in our Heavenly Father and in His plan can be a source of inner strength through which we can find peace, comfort, and the courage to cope. Faith is our anchor. As we put our faith and trust to work, hope is born. Hope grows out of faith and gives meaning and purpose to all that we do. It can give us comfort in the face of adversity, strength in times of trial, and peace when there is every reason for doubt and distress.

That is an incredible source of power available to all who love the Lord and who faithfully serve Him. That is the power I feel emanating from the women of the Church, all around the world.

President Spencer W. Kimball spoke a simple but profound truth when he stated, "Both a righteous man and a righteous woman are a blessing to all those whom their lives touch" (*My Beloved Sisters,* 37).

Every sister who stands for truth and righteousness diminishes the influence of evil. Every sister who strengthens and protects her family is doing the work of God. Every sister who lives as a woman of God becomes a beacon for others to follow and plants seeds of righteous influence that will be harvested for decades to come. Every sister who makes and keeps sacred covenants becomes an instrument in the hands of God.

I have been drawn to an interchange between God the Father and His Eldest and Only Begotten Son, who is the ultimate example of living up to one's premortal promises. When God asked who would come to earth to prepare a way for all mankind to be saved and strengthened and blessed, it was Jesus Christ who said, simply, "Here am I, send me" (Abraham 3:27).

Just as the Savior stepped forward to fulfill His divine responsibilities, so do we have the challenge and responsibility to do likewise. If you are wondering if you make a difference to the Lord, imagine the effect when you make commitments such as the following:

"Father, if you need a woman to rear children in righteousness, here am I, send me."

"If you need a woman to make a house, a home filled with love, here am I, send me." In so many instances and in so many ways, you are the emotional (and sometimes spiritual) glue that holds families together. Women live in homes under many different circumstances—married, single, widowed, divorced, some with children, and some without. But where the women are righteous and good, love, peace, and joy abound in the home. When children are in the home, every effort should be made by mothers to be home for them.

"If you need a woman who will shun vulgarity and dress modestly and speak with dignity and show the world how joyous it is to keep the commandments, here am I, send me."

"If you need a woman of faithful steadiness, here am I, send me."

Between now and the day the Lord comes again, He needs women in every family, in every ward, in every community, in every nation who will step forward in righteousness and say by their words and their actions, "Here am I, send me."

More than ever before, we need women anchored by faith, virtue, vision, and charity, as the Relief Society Declaration proclaims. We need women who can hear and will respond to the voice of the Lord, women who at all costs will defend and protect the family. We don't need women who want to be like men, sound like men, dress like men, drive like some men drive, or act like men. We do need women who rejoice in their womanhood and have a spiritual confirmation of their identity, their value, and their eternal destiny. Above all, we need women who will stand up for truth and righteousness and decry evil at every turn, women who will simply say, "Lord, here am I, send me."

CHAPTER 10

FOLLOWING
THE PROPHET

Many years ago, when I left on my mission to England, I was just another garden-variety young member of The Church of Jesus Christ of Latter-day Saints, although I suppose it was a bit unusual that the President of the Church attended my missionary farewell. President George Albert Smith said that his dear friend Elder Melvin J. Ballard, my late grandfather, had appeared to him in a dream and seemed to be quite disturbed about something. Consequently, President Smith called my father to see if there was a problem in the family, and my father told him that the only unusual thing going on in the family was my impending departure for the mission field. I was thrilled when President Smith came to my farewell and sat by me on the stand.

At the end of the meeting, the prophet embraced me and wished me well. I was touched by his kindness. Several months later I wrote to President Smith and among other things said, a bit brashly perhaps, "When you see my grandfathers, tell them I'm doing the best I can." In reading President Smith's response, I learned to expect the unexpected from the men the Lord has called to preside over His Church.

He wrote: "I'll tell them—if I see them before you do." Now, you need to realize that both my grandfathers had been dead for several years, and President Smith was much older than I. You can imagine that I was especially careful for the balance of my service in the mission field.

A few years ago at general conference, President Gordon B. Hinckley announced the construction of thirty new temples throughout the world. With seventeen temples at that time in various stages of planning and construction, this meant the Church was in the process of building forty-seven temples at one time, just four short of the total number of temples in operation at the time of the announcement. That didn't even count the two extra temples President Hinckley suggested we should add to the list "to make it an even 100 by the end of this century." When he said that, many of us chuckled, but our prophet was not joking.

He referred to this extraordinary temple-building effort as "a tremendous undertaking . . . the like of which we have never seen before." I can tell you in all honesty that in the months following the announcement, the enormous size of the task became more evident. The process of building even one temple is complex. Simply selecting the best site, obtaining the property, and securing all of the necessary permits and permissions have required months—even years—of concentrated effort by dozens of skilled professionals and ecclesiastical leaders. That doesn't include the time, energy, and resources required to design the temple; to retain contractors who are capable of the kind of craftsmanship building a house of the Lord demands; to build, furnish, and landscape appropriately; to plan and execute inspiring open house and dedicatory services; and to staff the temple adequately so that it functions and is maintained properly.

Now, multiply that effort by thirty and complicate the equation by figuring in the number of different languages, architectural conventions, and local building codes that must be considered, and you have some idea of the scope of this landmark temple-building endeavor. As President Hinckley said at the time of his announcement, "Nothing even approaching it has ever been tried before."

One might look at this remarkable expenditure of time and resources and wonder about its purpose. With fifty-one temples already in operation all around the world at the time, why go to all this trouble to nearly double that number in a relatively short period of time? After all, the construction of the Church's first fifty-three temples was spread out over the course of 168 years. Couldn't we have paced ourselves just a little?

President Hinckley, our inspired prophet-leader, senses an urgency to extend the blessings of temple worship to as many of our members as possible. As he explained, many of our members in remote areas of the world "have very little of this world's goods. But they have in their hearts a great burning faith concerning this latter-day work. They love the Church. They love the gospel. They love the Lord and want to do His will. They are paying their tithing, modest as it is. They make tremendous sacrifices to visit the temples. They travel for days at a time in cheap buses and on old boats. They save their money and do without to make it all possible. They need nearby temples—small, beautiful, serviceable temples. . . .

"If temple ordinances are an essential part of the restored gospel, and I testify that they are, then we must provide the means by which they can be accomplished. All of our vast family history endeavor is directed to temple work. There is no other purpose for it. The temple ordinances become the crowning blessings the Church has to offer" (*Ensign*, May 1998, 88).

At the same time, there is a spirit in the house of the Lord that exists nowhere else in the world. Those who worthily enter the temple to worship and to serve are invited to partake of a spiritual feast that provides sustenance for starving souls. It is appropriate that we do everything we can to provide that kind of uplift and motivation to our members, wherever they may be.

KEEPING PACE WITH THE PROPHET

In answer to the question about pacing ourselves a little, the fact of the matter is, we *are* pacing ourselves. The pace is the pace set by our beloved prophet. Anyone who has traveled with President Hinckley during the past few years knows that if you're going to keep up with him, you'd better be wearing running shoes. He has often mentioned that it is his intention to push as hard as he can for as long as he can. This is partially motivated by the work ethic that was instilled within him as a child and has continued as a key character trait throughout his life. To an even greater degree, it is motivated by a heightened sense of urgency that comes to many of the Lord's anointed as the full vision of His latter-day work is opened to them.

President Wilford Woodruff told of a visitation he received from the Prophet Joseph Smith some time after the Prophet was killed. According to President Woodruff's account of the experience, "[Joseph Smith] came to me and spoke to me. He said he could not stop to talk with me because he was in a hurry. The next man I met was Father Smith; he could not talk with me because he was in a hurry. I met half a dozen brethren who had held high positions on earth, and none of them could stop to talk with me because they were in a hurry. I was much astonished. By and by I saw the Prophet again and I got the privilege of asking him a question. 'Now,' said I, 'I want to know why you are in a hurry. I have been in a hurry all my life; but I expected my hurry would be over when I got into the kingdom of heaven, if I ever did.'

"Joseph said, 'I will tell you, Brother Woodruff. Every dispensation that has had the priesthood on the earth and has gone into the celestial kingdom has had a certain amount of work to do to prepare to go to the earth with the Savior when he goes to reign on the earth. Each dispensation has had ample time to do this work. We have not. We are the last dispensation, and so much work has to be done, and we need to be in a hurry to accomplish it.'

"Of course, that was satisfactory," President Woodruff concluded, "but it was new doctrine to me" (*Discourses of Wilford Woodruff*, 288–89).

Other latter-day prophets have been similarly motivated to move us along more quickly in accomplishing the significant work of this last great dispensation. President David O. McKay encouraged each member to be a missionary (*Man May Know for Himself*, 129). President Spencer W. Kimball urged us to "lengthen our stride" (*Ensign*, October 1974, 5). President Ezra Taft Benson said that the spirit of our work must be urgency (*Ensign*, May 1980, 32). President Howard W. Hunter reminded us: "This world needs the gospel of Jesus Christ. The gospel provides the only way the world will ever know peace. As followers of Jesus Christ, we seek to enlarge the circle of love and understanding among the people of the earth. . . . 'The harvest truly is great, but the labourers are few' . . . (Luke 10:2)" (*Ensign*, November 1994, 88). And now President Gordon B. Hinckley is asking us to "carry on," to do better, to do more. He has said: "We have a work to do, you and I, so very much of it. Let us roll up our sleeves and get at it, with a new commitment, putting our trust in the Lord. . . . We can do it, if we will be prayerful and faithful" (*Ensign*, May 1995, 87–88).

Clearly, the power of the Lord is moving upon the President of the Church, nudging him with the same spirit of urgency that seemed to be motivating Joseph Smith in Wilford Woodruff's vision. President Hinckley is doing all he can to accelerate the work. He is traveling the world to an unprecedented degree to strengthen and edify the Saints and to urge them upward and onward. He has made himself available to the world media, sometimes at great inconvenience, to share the message of the

Restoration with the widest possible audience. He is overseeing the most extensive era of temple building in history in an attempt to speed up our ability to accomplish the overwhelming amount of work we have been assigned to complete in this dispensation of time.

For us it is not a question of leadership, nor has it ever been. Throughout the entire history of the Church, our leaders have been dynamically out in front, leading the charge, showing the way. The question we must ask ourselves is, Are we keeping pace with our prophet? I can assure you that is a subject of considerable discussion among the members of the Quorum of the Twelve Apostles. That was the case with President Spencer W. Kimball, when I was first called to be an Apostle, and that is the case now with President Gordon B. Hinckley. Generally speaking, the Apostles are younger than the President of the Church. From my experience, we would like to think of ourselves as having been well conditioned for the rigors of the ministry, but we often find ourselves gasping for breath—spiritually and physically—as we push ourselves to follow our prophet's lead.

NO TIME TO RELAX

I hope the same is true of every council in every ward and stake of the Church and, indeed, for every member of the Church. This is not the time to coast in our callings. Every council and every member of the Church should be sprinting to match the pace of the prophet. There is much to be done to complete the work that must be completed in this dispensation. We must work harder and smarter if we are to accomplish our great eternal goals. As individuals and families, we need to examine ourselves and our personal commitment—particularly those of us who have made covenants of consecration and sacrifice in the house of the Lord.

Are we doing all we can do to keep pace with the prophet? Are we setting an example of Christian virtue and gospel faithfulness in our lives and in our homes? Are we reaching out to our inactive or nonmember friends, family members, and neighbors with loving concern? Are we boldly opening our mouths to share our testimonies? Are we serving with all our hearts and souls as home teachers and visiting teachers and in any other callings we may receive? Our leaders are doing these things. We can expect no less of ourselves if we want to keep our anchor and chain in top condition that we might be kept out of harm's way.

Some years ago there was a rather serious tragedy in our ward. A great woman, the wife of our former bishop and a woman beloved and respected in our ward family, contracted cancer of the worst kind. This was a vivacious, effervescent woman who lifted and inspired everyone she met. As the disease became worse, I gave her blessings. Other General Authorities gave her blessings. One of the blessings I gave was in the presence of her seventeen-year-old son. Another blessing was given to her when her son was eighteen. Our Heavenly Father, though, had something else in mind for her, and she was taken home to Him.

A few days after the funeral service, I visited the father. I put my arm around him and asked, "What can I do to help?"

His response was direct and heartfelt: "Help my son to understand."

Oh, how those words penetrated my mind. "What does he need to understand?" I asked.

"Why God would allow his dear mother to suffer the way she did," he said. "Russ, my son and my wife were the very best of friends. You have never seen a mother and son as close as they were. He loved her deeply. He prayed for her. He heard all the blessings that were given. He had faith that she would be healed—or, at the very least, would not have to suffer. Yet she suffered and died. He doesn't understand why."

For days I tried to get in touch with this young man. I called his home about twenty times without success. I finally wrote him a letter and invited him to have lunch with me at the Church Administration Building. I prayed that his heart would be touched to feel my love and concern. One Tuesday I returned to the office from a conference assignment, and my secretary informed me that my young neighbor and I had a lunch appointment for the following day.

He arrived the next day exactly on time. We went down to the General Authority lunchroom. As we sat there, eating and chatting, six Apostles came in for lunch. Now, I must tell you that I've eaten lunch there many times, and I've rarely seen six of the Twelve there at the same time. One by one, all six came over to the table where we were sitting to greet us.

Elder Monson (this was before he was called to the First Presidency) stopped at our table. This tall, powerful Apostle reached over and ruffled my young friend's hair just a bit and said, "Are you getting this young man ready for a mission, Russ?" At the time this young man was not prepared to hear about serving a mission. Two of the other members of the Twelve greeted us in a similar way. I could see my neighbor squirm a little each time.

After lunch, we went up to my office. For ninety minutes I tried to answer some of the questions that had been troubling him since his mother's death. It isn't easy to explain to a boy who adored his mother why priesthood blessings didn't heal her. He couldn't understand. He was struggling inwardly. I don't know that what I said did much good, but we had a nice visit together. As we walked out of my office to go toward the elevator, we saw that Elder L. Tom Perry's office door was open. We could see him sitting behind his desk. I knocked on his door and asked, "May I introduce you to a friend of mine?"

He said, "Yes, come in."

"Elder Perry," I said. "This is my neighbor. He lost his mother just recently. She died of cancer, and he's having a hard time understanding spiritually why his mother had to die the way she did."

Then Elder Perry—and I'll love him all the days of my life for what he did—wrapped his hands around my friend's hand and looked him right in the eye (this took some doing, because Elder Perry is about six-feet, four-inches tall). He said, "My boy, I understand exactly how you feel. I lost my wife two years ago with the same disease. Now, son, you must keep the eternal perspective." And then he taught him, as beautifully as I have ever heard, the eternal nature of man in a matter of a few minutes. It was a remarkable sermon, simply and powerfully stated, and I could see it had an effect on my neighbor.

We left and walked down the hallway. By this time we had met seven of the Apostles. As we turned the corner, out walked Elder David B. Haight, the eighth Apostle we had met. I've gone several days at a time without seeing that many Apostles around Church headquarters, and here we were seeing them within a matter of an hour or two. Elder Haight came up, put his arm around this young man, and asked, "Getting ready to go on a mission?" By this time my friend had no idea how to respond. He just gulped. Hard.

We got on the elevator and went down to the basement to walk to the parking lot. In the elevator I took hold of his arm and said to him, "Your mother knows you are here, and your mother is a good friend of the Lord's. It is because of her that you are having this experience. We all love you, son. Try to keep the eternal perspective."

As we stepped off the elevator, we saw President Kimball walk through the back doors of the Church Administration Building. I was holding onto my friend's arm, and I felt a physical jolt hit him when he saw the prophet. It was as though somebody had touched him with a live electrical wire. We stood there a minute silently. Finally, he looked at me and asked, "Brother Ballard, does President Kimball ever see somebody like me?"

"I don't know," I said. "Let's find out."

We went back into the Church Administration Building and called Arthur Haycock, who was President Kimball's secretary. I explained to him the situation and asked if the prophet would have a minute to see us. Brother Haycock invited us to come right up. As busy as President Kimball was, he was going to take the time for a boy who was struggling.

We walked into his office. President Kimball got up from his desk and walked around to greet us. He took hold of my neighbor's hands and looked deeply into his eyes—and into his heart.

"My boy," he said, "your mother is all right."

Can you imagine having the prophet of the Lord answer your question that personally and that directly? It was an extraordinary moment for my young friend—and for me.

President Kimball invited my neighbor to sit and talk with him. They talked about "Tragedy or Destiny?" a great sermon President Kimball had delivered when he was an Apostle. It was given at the time of a terrible airplane accident in which nearly fifty members of the Mormon Tabernacle Choir were killed. All around the Church people were asking why the Lord would allow such a thing to happen. President Kimball tried to answer why in this great sermon, which was published in pamphlet form. Now, he produced a copy of that pamphlet and wrote on the inside cover: "To [my friend], Affectionately, Spencer W. Kimball," and handed it to him.

Then he taught us a great lesson I will never forget. He said, "My boy, I've had some difficult times in my life. I didn't like the idea of having my vocal cords operated on. I didn't want that to happen. I didn't like the idea of being opened up when I was in my late seventies to have my heart worked on. But let me tell you something. Through my suffering, I have come to know God." Then President Kimball took hold of my friend, drew him close, and gave him a hug. Then he gave me a hug.

My friend and I turned to leave. Just as we were walking out the door, President Kimball called after us, "When you return from your mission, young man, you will understand more of what I am saying."

Fifteen minutes later we were standing in the parking lot, reflecting on the experience we had just shared.

"Did you hear what the President said to you?" I asked. "Did you really hear?"

"Oh, Brother Ballard, he said so much . . ."

"But did you hear what he said about a mission?" I pressed. "He said, 'When you return from your mission, you will understand.'

"Of course, President Kimball has asked every worthy young man to go on a mission," I continued. "But you have been called specifically, so I think you have a lot to do. Instead of going back to work today, I think you need to go home so you can privately ponder and pray during the rest of the afternoon about what has happened."

That is just what he did. Another neighbor told me that she took dinner over to the family, and when my friend came to the door she could see that he was emotionally drained.

"What in the world has happened?" she asked.

"Oh, come in," he said. "The most wonderful thing happened to me today. I've learned for myself that my mother is all right and that the one who is sick is me."

Just a few months later, I had the great pleasure of standing before a gathering of the First Presidency, the Quorum of the Twelve Apostles and other General Authorities in the Salt Lake Temple and announcing that our young friend had, that very morning, entered the Missionary Training Center en route to his mission. President Kimball looked at me, and we shared a smile. By following the counsel of a living prophet, my young friend's faith was strengthened, once again becoming an anchor in his life.

"LET US GO FORWARD"

Our latter-day prophets have warned us of our sobering obligation to prepare for "the great and dreadful day of the Lord" (D&C 2:1). There is still much to be done. It is a day of urgency in the Lord's work. Our prophet is picking up the pace. We must be prepared to keep up with him, stride for lengthened stride.

As we strive to lengthen our stride, I cannot emphasize enough the importance of following the prophet and the Apostles. In today's world, where twenty-four hours a day the media's talking heads spew forth conflicting opinions, where men and women jockey for everything from your money to your vote, there is one clear, unpolluted, unbiased voice that you can always count on. And that is the voice of the living prophet and the Apostles. Their only motive is "the everlasting welfare of your souls" (2 Nephi 2:30).

Think of it! Think about the value of having a source of information you can always count on, that will always have your eternal interests at heart, and that will always provide inspired truth. That's a phenomenal gift and guide, a wonderful strong link we can rely on.

CHAPTER 11

FOCUSING
ON THE FAMILY

As we work to strengthen the links in the chain that connects us to our anchor of faith, one of the first things we realize is that we cannot do it alone. "Nevertheless neither is the man without the woman, neither the woman without the man, in the Lord," counseled the Apostle Paul (1 Corinthians 11:11). From the inspired document "The Family: A Proclamation to the World" come these words of living prophets and Apostles:

"The family is ordained of God. Marriage between man and woman is essential to His eternal plan. Children are entitled to birth within the bonds of matrimony, and to be reared by a father and a mother who honor marital vows with complete fidelity. Happiness in family life is most likely to be achieved when founded upon the teachings of the Lord Jesus Christ. Successful marriages and families are established and maintained on principles of faith, prayer, repentance, forgiveness, respect, love, compassion, work, and wholesome recreational activities" (*Ensign,* November 1995, 102).

Some years ago two ministers came to Salt Lake City at the invitation of the First Presidency. I was assigned, along with

Bishop Robert D. Hales of the Presiding Bishopric, to host these two fine men. They had come to Salt Lake City because they were concerned about declining activity among the members of their church. They concluded that one of the things they needed to do to improve activity among their members was to focus more attention upon the family. As they examined what was going on around the world among other faith groups, they concluded that the organization that best understood the family was The Church of Jesus Christ of Latter-day Saints. And so they came to Salt Lake to gather materials and to be instructed and to see what they could learn from us that they could put to work within their own church.

We were delighted to meet with them and to respond to all of their questions and requests. We took them to all the departments of the Church that had anything to do with the family. In the evening we hosted a dinner for them on the tenth floor of the Joseph Smith Memorial Building. By that time they had gathered so much material that they had to have it shipped back home in boxes. They couldn't carry all the manuals, videotapes, TV commercials, and other materials we had prepared for them relative to our work with the families of the Church—and the world.

At the conclusion of the dinner, one of these gentlemen said to me: "Mr. Ballard, we cannot thank you enough for your courtesy and all that you have shared with us. We are very anxious to take these things back now and implement them into the activities of our church."

I assured him that it was an honor to be able to share with him some of the materials that we had. "But I would be less than honest," I added, "if I did not tell you one thing."

"What is that?" my new friend asked.

"Those materials will never work for you like they work for us," I said.

He seemed a little surprised by my statement. "Oh?" he asked. "Why is that?"

"Because your concept of the family is very, very different from our concept of the family," I said. He seemed puzzled, so I tried to illustrate my concern.

"Do you perform marriages?" I asked him.

"I do," he said. He gestured toward his companion, adding, "We both do."

"When you perform a marriage, do you have language in the ceremony indicating that the husband and wife are married until they are parted by death?"

"Yes, we have that language in our marriage ceremony," he acknowledged.

"So in effect, when you marry a couple you also make a pronouncement of divorce at death," I said. "Not so in The Church of Jesus Christ of Latter-day Saints."

From where we were dining, we had a lovely view of the Salt Lake Temple. I motioned toward it and said, "In that temple across the street, those who have the authority of the priesthood of God perform marriages for time and for all eternity. Couples are sealed, or bound together, by the same authority that Jesus Christ gave to Peter and the Apostles of old.

"Therefore," I continued, "the family in The Church of Jesus Christ of Latter-day Saints is conceptually different from the family in any other organization. When a man is bound to his wife, sealed by the power of the holy priesthood for time and all eternity, and children are born under that covenant, they understand that their family can be together forever."

I paused for a moment, allowing that doctrinal concept to sink in. "Can you see how that understanding would make a difference in how people feel about their family?" I asked. "It's not just about here and now—it's about forever. If you're making a commitment forever, it's more likely to be a high priority to you, requiring your full attention and focus.

"So it isn't really our programs that make our families work," I explained. "Oh, the programs are inspired and wonderful, and they really do make a difference for us. But the thing that really matters here is the doctrine. That's what makes the programs work. Without the doctrinal foundation of the eternal nature of the family unit, the programs are just good ideas that may help you but won't really make a difference for your church—at least, not in the way you are hoping."

I wasn't trying to discourage our visitors. I'm sure our programs have been helpful to them. There are good and wonderful people all around the world who care deeply about their families and are doing significant things in behalf of parents and children everywhere. The Church of Jesus Christ of Latter-day Saints is not alone in its respect, reverence, and appreciation for the family as the fundamental unit of society. But we are alone among the world's religions in understanding the family's eternal possibilities and in performing sacred ordinances that bind family members to each other not just for time but for all eternity.

TEACHING OUR CHILDREN TODAY FOR TOMORROW

Have you seen the future when you gazed through the hospital nursery window and watched a bassinet being wheeled into view? You see that beautiful newborn infant for the first time. A new spirit comes into your life as your son or daughter or grandchild, and you know that your life will never be quite the same again. How often have you had to blink back the tears as you stood in awe and contemplated the miracle of a new life? This newly arrived spirit has come in sweet innocence from the presence of God. Every human being is a spirit child of God and lived with Heavenly Father before coming to earth. He entrusts His spirit children to earthly parents, who provide a mortal body for them through the miracle of physical birth. He gives to parents the sacred opportunity and responsibility to love, protect, teach, and bring up children in light and truth so they may one day, through the Atonement and the Resurrection of Jesus Christ, return to our Father's presence.

These precious souls come to us in purity and innocence. As parents we assume an immense responsibility for their care and well-being. Although we share this sacred trust with brothers and sisters, aunts and uncles, grandparents, teachers, neighbors, and all who touch the lives and impress or influence the souls of these precious children, we cannot abdicate our responsibility as parents. We cannot and we must not allow the school, community, television, or even Church organizations to establish our children's values. The Lord has placed this duty with mothers and fathers. It is one from which we cannot escape and one that cannot be delegated. Parents remain accountable. Therefore, we must guard the sanctity of our homes, because that is where children develop their values, attitudes, and habits for everyday living.

King Benjamin admonished parents many years ago, "But ye will teach them to walk in the ways of truth and soberness; ye will teach them to love one another, and to serve one another" (Mosiah 4:15).

The critical nature of the first tender, formative years cannot be overstated. Our little ones are like seedlings in a plant nursery. All look much the same in the beginning, but each one grows to become independent and unique. Parents are to nourish, tend, and teach their children so that they will grow to their full stature and potential.

Parents should see beyond the little girl in pigtails and should not be misled by the ragged little boy with a dirty face and holes in the knees of his pants. Visionary parents see children as they may become. They see the valiant missionary who will one day share his testimony with the world and later become a righteous father who honors his priesthood. The inspired grandparent sees pure and beautiful mothers and future presidents of the Relief Society, Young Women, and Primary, even though today they may be girls who giggle and chatter during family home evening. Sometimes we hear people chuckle as they say, "Well, boys will be boys!" In reality, boys will be men, and almost before we know it. To see our children grow, succeed, and take their places in society and in the Lord's kingdom is an eternal reward worth any inconvenience or sacrifice.

Oh, that every parent could understand that children come from a premortal experience and have possibilities that often are far beyond what we might expect. We are charged to help them reach their full potential. Is it any wonder that Jesus brought the little children unto Himself to teach and bless them? He said, "Whosoever shall receive one of such children in my name, receiveth me" (Mark 9:37). He also said, "It is not the will of your Father which is in heaven, that one of these little ones should perish" (Matthew 18:14).

When asked who is the greatest in the kingdom of heaven, the Savior "called a little child unto him, and set him in the midst of them, and said, Verily I say unto you, Except ye be converted, and become as little children, ye shall not enter into the kingdom of heaven. Whosoever therefore shall humble himself as this little child, the same is greatest in the kingdom of heaven" (Matthew 18:1–4).

"Can I Go Too?"

One Saturday morning I was preparing for an activity with one of my grandsons. Before we could make our way out the door, I heard another small voice inquiring, "Can I go too, Grandpa?"

Have you ever tried to say no to such a request? Our activity would not have been the same without that someone else who really wanted to "go too."

Just as surely, heaven will not be heaven if some of our

children who want to "go too" are left behind. We have the task of helping them learn about our Heavenly Father's plan for us, demonstrating our faith in the Lord, and continuing to work with our children in prayerful and patient persuasion so that they may choose to become worthy participants in the Father's plan. Our testimonies must be strong enough to anchor them until they have forged a firm anchor of their own.

To teach our children the gospel of Jesus Christ and to protect them from the influences of a wicked world, love must abide in our homes. We should cherish and care for our children with unwavering dedication. The older we grow, the more precious our family becomes to us. We come to see more clearly that all of the wealth, honor, and positions of the world pale in significance when compared to the precious souls of our loved ones.

What a beautiful place this world will be when all fathers and mothers see the importance of teaching their children the principles that will help them be happy and successful. Parents teach best when they lead by good example, govern their little ones with patience, kindness, and love unfeigned, and demonstrate the same love for children that Jesus exemplified.

Our children do not grow to full physical stature suddenly. We measure their growth in inches. In like manner, their spiritual growth takes place over time, as link by gospel link is formed and then strengthened by life's experiences. This development might also be compared to erecting a block building. The walls are formed block by block with a strong mortar holding each block to the others. We could give these building blocks such names as sharing stories at bedtime, listening to a child pray, or tucking a child into bed at night with a good-night kiss. Other blocks could be pleasant dinner conversations, praise for tasks well done, birthday parties, and family outings. Still others might include doing chores, being kind to one another, reading from the scriptures together, serving others, and saying "I love you." Additional blocks might be learning to work and take responsibility, respecting our leaders and those who are older, singing together, doing homework, attending Primary, and honoring the Sabbath day.

Even larger blocks are family home evening, respecting and honoring the priesthood, and family prayer. A vast array of these building blocks, placed carefully, can form a fortress of faith that the tidal waves of worldly distraction and evil cannot breach. These blocks are held together with a mortar called love: love of Heavenly Father and His Son Jesus Christ, love of parents, love for each other, love for choosing the good.

THE POWER OF PRAYER IN FAMILIES

In addition to family prayers, other prayers can be of great benefit to families, parents, and children. For parents, there is nothing quite like that wonderful moment at the end of the day when you can kneel together and hold hands and pray together as husband and wife, mother and father. If you have fallen out of that habit, return to it—tonight! What I am asking you to do is to have that prayer—just Mom and Dad alone at the end of the day, holding each other's hand. It is a great time to thank the Lord for your companion and for your children and for one more day together. If you sense a special need that your companion or one of your children may have, it is a great time to ask Heavenly Father for guidance on that matter.

My wife and I have had that practice for more than fifty years. When it is her night to pray, it is a simple, wonderful prayer; and when it is mine, I hope it is the same. It is my fervent testimony that Lucifer cannot penetrate a marriage, cannot cause disagreement and misunderstanding, cannot fill the bishops' offices in this Church with members whose marriages are racked with misunderstanding and pain, when we take time to pray together as couples. I believe that that one simple act of going to our knees and holding hands and calling down the blessings of God into our homes and into our marriages can do more than all of the counseling that might be made available to us. Why? Because God is our Father. We are His children. He loves us. If we show our faith in Him by calling down the blessings of heaven into our marriages, every single night, He will help us get from where we are to where we would like to be.

At least, that has been my experience. When a couple comes to me for counsel relative to various struggles in their marriage, one of the first questions I ask them is, "Do you kneel together at the end of the day and hold hands and say your prayers?" Interestingly, not once—not once—has the answer to that question been positive. Then I suggest, "Will you please go home and do that for the next thirty days? Then you can return and we will talk again." Almost always the couples come back and, with tears in their eyes, share with me the sweet feelings that have returned to their marriages and how they think, at last, that they are going to make it. Such is the power of prayer in strengthening and maintaining marriages and families.

Similarly, for a young person who is struggling, who perhaps feels Mom and Dad don't understand, I urge you to learn to pray this way: "Heavenly Father, help me to communicate with Mom and Dad." Don't try to get through mortality without turning to your Heavenly Father who has loved you and cherished you and cradled you eons of time longer than your earthly parents. They who kneel before the Lord and call upon Heavenly Father in the name of the Lord Jesus Christ for guidance and help—and then listen—will receive a feeling within the bosom that will guide them.

We must not try to have great, eternal families without making our Heavenly Father an integral part of them. We are entitled to call down the blessings of heaven within the great institution of the family. And Father, never hesitate in times of need to bless your wife and your children through the righteous exercise of your priesthood. This, too, will draw the powers of heaven into their lives to fortify them against the evil one.

CALMLY, KINDLY, PEACEFULLY

Some years ago I had the privilege of being bishop of the ward in which Elder LeGrand Richards lived. This was at the time when it seemed that everyone who wanted to get married in the temple wanted Brother Richards to perform the ceremony. As bishop of the ward, I heard him speak to many young couples in the temple sealing rooms. He used to tell of a man who was ninety-five years of age and in vigorous health. Somebody came to him one day and asked, "To what do you attribute your vigor and your strength at such a great age?"

The response: "Well, when my wife and I got married, we agreed that we would never, ever argue. If there was ever an argument brewing, I would just step outside for a few minutes until things calmed down. And spending most of my life outside is why I am in such good health."

Brother Richards used this illustration to teach these young couples that it is better to step outside for a moment until things calm down than to allow the spirit of contention, whose author is Lucifer, to find a foothold within the walls of our homes. You will not teach nor cradle nor weld together a celestial family in anger.

I know that there will occasionally be tension in the home. Things happen in our day-to-day lives that prompt misunderstanding and irritation. Sometimes these frustrations are major, life-altering issues; more often they are small and petty but still annoying, like a tiny pebble in your shoe. For whatever reason, contemporary society has conditioned us to believe that anger and rage are appropriate, or at least understandable, reactions to these annoyances. Some would even contend that there is something wrong with a family in which these feelings are not occasionally expressed. A friend of mine, a fine father and grandfather, puts it this way: "Any parent who hasn't at least considered mayhem as a child-raising technique isn't really paying attention."

Though I understand that sentiment, in my view it is contrary to the loving gospel spirit that should permeate our homes and families. I have counseled fathers that they should be very careful how they preside over the affairs within the walls of their own home. If they have a temper or a short fuse or a tendency to raise their voice and be angry and disagreeable within the walls of their own home, they need to get over it. Where there is anger, where there is ugliness of words, where tempers are flaring, you will not have the solidarity and the strength and the power of the kind of homes that we must have to be able to raise our families and to see them safely through the years that lie ahead.

The same is true of the sisters. If you have a short fuse, if you have a tendency to lose your cool, please repent. Put that behind you. After teaching this principle, I have had sisters come to me and say, "Brother Ballard, if you had my children, you would understand that you are asking me to do the impossible." Well, I don't know what kind of children you have, probably pretty good ones, but regardless of the circumstance or the provocation, you need to remain calm. Keep things under control within the walls of your own home.

Barbara and I have raised seven children. I wish I could tell you that those seven children have never heard their father lose his cool, but that wouldn't be true, although there hasn't been much of it for the past twenty-five years or so. Thank heaven for repentance! But if you were to ask them, "Have you ever heard your mother raise her voice?" all seven would say, "No." And they adore her as I do. Why? Because there has been a spirit of calmness in our home even when there have been traumatic, difficult challenges in raising children.

Children also have a responsibility to assist in maintaining a peaceful home environment. When I speak of children, I am talking about any that are still living in the home of their parents. You do not have the right ever to be disrespectful to your mother or your father. Period. If you haven't had that taught to you before, write it in your journal and in your minds and hearts right now. Write down that I said you do not have the right to be ugly, to raise your voice, to slam doors, to scream or holler within the walls of your own home. Young people, you do have the right to be heard. If you are having difficulty getting your mother and your father to listen to you, in a calm manner just ask: "Mom and Dad, I've got a different feeling about a matter. Can we set a time to talk about it?" Sometimes family home evening is a wonderful time for parents and children to calmly talk about matters, to try to come to a better understanding of differing points of view.

I learned a lesson years ago from our oldest daughter. She was about four at the time. She came into the room all excited. I was reading the newspaper, and she had something very much on her mind that was very important to her. I was responding, "Yes, uh-huh, uh-huh."

All of a sudden, the newspaper came crashing down with her two little hands. She grabbed my face and whipped it around so that we had eye-to-eye contact. This is a little four-year-old teaching her father a great lesson. "Daddy, you're not listening to me."

And she was right. Now if you need to do that, do it gently and wisely, but get your father's and your mother's attention so that you can talk about those things that are on your mind, that you are challenged with, that you are struggling with.

Throughout the history of Heavenly Father's dealings with His mortal children, the voice of heaven has been a still, small voice. "Be still," wrote the psalmist, "and know that I am God" (Psalm 46:10). Christ came to bring peace to our hearts and to our homes. Said He, "Peace I leave with you, my peace I give unto you: not as the world giveth, give I unto you. Let not your heart be troubled, neither let it be afraid" (John 14:27).

Is it possible to have that peaceful feeling in our homes and families all of the time? Certainly President David O. McKay felt that it was. He and his beloved wife, Emma, both noted on many occasions that a harsh word had never passed between them. Any who saw these two sweethearts could vouch for the tender peacefulness that always seemed to exist in their presence.

I also know it is possible to have that kind of spirit in your home. I've seen it and felt it in my own home and in the homes of others I have visited all around the world on my various Church assignments. It can and does exist if you learn to be careful in your relationships with each other. Be kind and thoughtful and patient and forgiving. Do not abuse one another in any way—physically, emotionally, or otherwise. There is no place in the calm, peaceful, loving home for any kind of abuse. And please remember: sometimes silence is as deafeningly abusive as lashing out with an uncontrolled tongue. Please don't manipulate your loved ones in that way. Whether abuse is physical, verbal, or the less evident but equally severe emotional abuse, it is an abomination and a serious offense to God. Jesus left no question about the seriousness of harming children in any way when he said, "But whoso shall offend one of these little ones which believe in me, it were better for him that a millstone were hanged about his neck, and that he were drowned in the depth of the sea" (Matthew 18:6).

If there are issues or concerns, talk about them—calmly, kindly, peacefully. Look for answers, not rebuttal; solutions, not revenge; peace, not conquest.

THE ROLE AND REACH OF EXTENDED FAMILIES

Other family members can and do have impact on the lives of young children. Many children have only one parent at home, and some are left with no parents at all. We all share a responsibility to help fill such voids and to provide sustained assistance and encouragement.

At this point in my life, when my heart—and sometimes home—are filled with the happy voices of beautiful grandchildren, I am especially mindful of the significant role extended family members can play. Brothers and sisters, aunts and uncles, grandparents and cousins can all make a powerful difference.

The role and reach of grandparents is especially profound. I think one of the assignments we have as grandparents is to make memories for our grandchildren, memories that will live with them long after we are gone. And I hope you grandchildren are looking for opportunities to be around your grandparents.

I recognize that some do not have grandparents living nearby, and you do not have the privilege of spending time with them. Perhaps some of them are now deceased. That was the case with my mother's parents. They had both died before I was born, and so I never had the opportunity to meet Grandfather or Grandmother Smith. Meeting them is one of the things I look forward to. But I have tried to understand everything I can about those grandparents. I have learned as I have studied about their lives that they were mighty in the kingdom of God. They loved the Lord, and they devoted their lives to the building of the kingdom. I hope you will do the same to learn everything you can about your grandparents.

My Grandfather Ballard died when I was ten years of age. I really didn't know him as an Apostle; I just knew him as Grandpa. I wish now that I had learned then a little more about who he was and what his marvelous assignment was. But I am so grateful that Grandpa Ballard made a memory for me that I will never forget. It was on my eighth birthday, and he took me to the old Rialto Theater in Salt Lake City. I was really excited about going with Grandpa to the movies. As soon as the lights went off and the film started, Grandpa Ballard fell fast asleep.

As I recall, he slept rather noisily. I kept looking around, wondering if he was disturbing the people in the theater. He slept right through the whole movie. In fact, I had to wake him up at the end. I couldn't believe it. How could anybody sleep through a Walt Disney movie?

Much later in my life, about five years after being called as a General Authority, I understood. I came home from a long and heavy weekend, and for family home evening, Barbara had planned to take our children to see a movie at the Center Theater. We sat down, the lights went off, and I fell sound asleep. To this day my children cannot understand how it was possible for their father to sleep through *Star Wars*. Through that experience I learned that it is an occupational hazard in the life of a General Authority that whenever lights go out, he goes out with them. But my having a grandfather who found time to take me to a movie, even though he slept through it, has been a lasting memory.

I hope you don't underestimate the power of a memory such as that in the lives of your grandchildren. And I hope you don't underestimate your potential influence in teaching significant gospel lessons to your grandchildren.

Another memory I have of Grandfather Ballard concerns one of his rare visits to my father's cabin in Lamb's Canyon, east of Salt Lake City. Grandfather had a great love for the Indians; he had worked with them for ten years as president of the Northwestern States Mission from 1909 to 1919. One Saturday he took us children into some trees away from the cabin. He said, "I want to build for you a kiva." We were anxious to know what a kiva was. He told us that the Indians of the Northwest built seats in the trees where they could sit and have a council meeting. "We will build a kiva, and then we will have a council meeting." My grandfather built very primitive little seats, and the grandchildren who were there sat and held a meeting.

I have cherished those memories all of these years. My

counsel to you is to find ways in which you can be one-on-one with your grandchildren and make a memory. If you haven't made a memory recently in the life of your grandchildren, I pray that the Lord will touch your mind to think of what you might uniquely do as one of the most important teachers that your grandchildren may ever have in mortality—perhaps just the penning of a little note or making a phone call to a grandchild can make a memory. Certainly a hug and a warm expression of love will create a lasting memory in the heart of any child.

I hope that we are taking opportunities to touch one another's lives and to do little, simple things to make meaningful memories that will live on and on. At some point such memories may even cause a child or a grandchild to have the courage and the strength to move past temptation and other difficulties they will face in their lives because of the connection that was made between them and their parents or their grandparents. We need to make lasting memories in the lives of our children.

It may not always be the parent or the grandparent who provides the right influence at a critical time. Sometimes it is a favorite aunt or uncle who is the miracle in a child's life; sometimes it is a brother or sister. I recently learned of a teenager who was having trouble being responsible about schoolwork. The parents cajoled and threatened. When homework wasn't done, the young woman was grounded or lost other privileges. Nothing seemed to work. Then one day in conversation with an aunt, this teenager asked when her aunt was going to take her on a special trip. The response? "When you get all A's and B's for a whole year." The challenge was accepted, and the young woman's report cards were totally transformed. The two of them took a fun vacation trip together.

As family members, may we take every opportunity to teach each other those things that will help us be strong in our faith, that we may not drift into temptation's path. May we hold tight to the iron rod, which will help us make our way back into the presence of our Father in Heaven.

I am reminded of an experience I had not long ago. A few weeks after I spoke at a stake conference, one of the sisters who had attended came up to me at another function and said, "Brother Ballard, I would like to tell you something." I responded that I am always eager to learn and asked what she wanted to tell me.

She said, "My little boy attended stake conference with our family. You were the visiting General Authority. My son has a habit that after anything special happens in his life, the first thing he wants to do when he gets home is to call his grandfather, my father, who lives in a distant city, and tell him about his experience. When we got home from the stake conference, he started pestering me to call Grandpa. I dialed the number and handed the phone to him. Here is how he greeted his grandfather: 'Grandpa, Grandpa, guess what happened to me today!' I suppose Dad responded with something like 'I don't know. Tell me.' My son said, 'I heard an old fossil today.'"

Now, I am not really an "old fossil," although that's what the boy understood when he heard me described as an "Apostle." But that isn't what's important here. What is important is that a little boy could hardly wait to share special happenings with his grandfather. Truly, "love is the chain whereby to bind a child to his parents" and his grandparents (Francis B. Carpenter, in *Bartlett's Familiar Quotations*, 524).

CONCLUSION

PRESSING FORWARD

S everal years ago I had a frightening experience while flying from Reno, Nevada, to San Rafael, California, with a friend in his twin-engine Aztec airplane. The weather was a little cloudy when we left Reno, and my friend was somewhat worried about it. Because of his concern, we landed at the Lake Tahoe airport to get a second report on the weather. It did not indicate that the weather was too bad, so we continued our flight to San Rafael.

Our destination was an airport in the northern part of San Francisco. As we approached the Bay area, the clouds became increasingly low and dense. We tried to stay under the clouds so we could see the water and thus keep our bearings visually. But suddenly we flew into very dense clouds and fog and could see nothing.

When you fly into such clouds, you can become totally disoriented. You do not know whether you are flying straight, sideways, or upside down. You lose your sense of forward motion, and it takes a few minutes for the pilot to orient himself from visual flying to instrument flying. At 180 miles an hour, you move a long distance in a few minutes and can get into serious trouble quickly. Unfortunately, my friend had not flown entirely on instruments for some time.

He struggled to get his bearings and was near panic as he tried to recall all that he had learned about instrument flying. I knew very little about instrument flying, so I could not help him. All I could do was put my hand on his shoulder and tell him to take a deep breath and get hold of himself. The only instrument I could read was the altimeter. I said to him, as calmly as I could, "We are now at five hundred feet. Don't make any quick moves; just think it out, and you can pull us through." Then I continued to pray and exercise all my faith, seeking help from the Lord.

My friend knew that the plane was completely out of control and that our chances of pulling out of this danger were marginal. We could easily go the wrong way. The foothills, buildings, towers, ocean, and bridges were not far away. At one time we dropped to only two hundred feet and must have been flying upside down because the maps and other items in the visor above my head fell into my lap.

At the peak of this crisis, an instant replay of my entire life flashed through my mind. I thought of my wife, my children, my parents, my business partners, the thirty-seven priests to whom I was then adviser, and many other things. I prayed urgently all through this crisis and made a commitment more deep and more sincere than ever before in my life.

"Heavenly Father," I pleaded, "guide us out of this thick, dense cloud, and help my friend remember all he knows about instrument flying." I committed to Heavenly Father that if He would help us, I would place my life in His hands. I promised Him that I would be what He wanted me to be.

It seemed an eternity before my friend finally made radio contact with Hamilton Air Force Base. He said, "I am in trouble; please help me."

The air traffic controllers had us on their radar screen and immediately began to help my friend regain control of the plane. They told us where we were and started to give us instructions to help guide us to safety.

When my friend heard the voice from Hamilton Tower, he regained a sense of confidence that enabled him to pull himself together.

Finally, we saw the lights on the runway. The white line in the center of the runway was a most welcome sight, and the rumble of solid ground under our airplane's wheels was among the most comforting sensations I have ever experienced.

Never in my life have I felt such intense urgency as I did during those few moments of in-flight emergency. Lives were at stake. Long-term effects on me and on those nearest and dearest to me hung in the balance. My anchor of faith in the Lord Jesus Christ was all that I had to lean on.

THE SPIRIT OF URGENCY

I've thought about that intense, urgent feeling many times since then. As I have served in the holy Apostleship, I have come close to that feeling as Heavenly Father has opened the eyes of my understanding to the peril facing His children if we do not take this great latter-day work seriously. I have been inspired as I have struggled to keep pace with President Gordon B. Hinckley, who is clearly motivated by a heightened sense of urgency.

To a great degree, the same is true for all of us in our respective callings and assignments—especially our most significantly sacred callings within the walls of our own homes as we continue our personal search for happiness and peace. The more we learn of our Heavenly Father's plan for His children, the more we feel the urgency to intensify our search—for ourselves and for others.

The prayerful experience of Enos in the Book of Mormon is instructive in this regard. Remember, Enos was a grandson of

Father Lehi. You get the feeling that perhaps he had not been as valiant throughout his life as he could have been. For some reason, out in the wilderness, surrounded by God's creations, the words and teachings of his father, Jacob, suddenly distilled on his soul and sank deep into his heart.

Enos wrote: "And my soul hungered; and I kneeled down before my Maker, and I cried unto him in mighty prayer and supplication." At first Enos was moved to pray "for mine own soul." Then, after he had prayed all day long, a voice came to him, saying, "Enos, thy sins are forgiven thee, and thou shalt be blessed." Enos recorded, "And I, Enos, knew that God could not lie; wherefore, my guilt was swept away" (Enos 1:4–6).

With that assurance through the atoning sacrifice of the Lord Jesus Christ, Enos then started praying in behalf of his brethren, the Nephites. He continued to search in the light of Christ until he received assurances from the Lord regarding them. Then he started praying on behalf of his enemies, the Lamanites.

Do you see how it works? Our search for happiness and our search for spiritual growth is an ongoing search—for ourselves, for our families, for our friends, and even for those who are not friendly toward us. Once we have found peace and happiness for ourselves by being "spiritually . . . born of God" with "his image in [our] countenances" and a "mighty change in [our] hearts" (Alma 5:14), the Spirit naturally moves our hearts and thoughts toward others. It begins with those closest to us and eventually extends through miles of distance and generations of time so that we might help others along the way in their own search, for "it becometh every man who hath been warned to warn his neighbor" (D&C 88:81).

Sadly, there are many in the Church who feel their search is over once they have gained a testimony and performed temple ordinances for themselves. Others feel that some searching and service must be done, but that once they reach a certain age or level of Church experience, they can "retire." I find myself wondering if we are all following the same prophet or reading the same scriptures:

"He that endureth to the end shall be saved" (Matthew 10:22).

"And if they endure unto the end they shall be lifted up at the last day, and shall be saved in the everlasting kingdom of the Lamb" (1 Nephi 13:37).

"Look unto me, and endure to the end, and ye shall live; for unto him that endureth to the end will I give eternal life" (3 Nephi 15:9).

"And, if you keep my commandments and endure to the end you shall have eternal life, which gift is the greatest of all the gifts of God" (D&C 14:7).

"Continue in these things even unto the end, and you shall have a crown of eternal life at the right hand of my Father, who is full of grace and truth" (D&C 66:12).

Near the end of his extraordinary sermon to his people, King Benjamin expressed his sense of urgency—and the need to stay faithful right to the end—with these powerful words: "And finally, I cannot tell you all the things whereby ye may commit sin; for there are divers ways and means, even so many that I cannot number them. But this much I can tell you, that if ye do not watch yourselves, and your thoughts, and your words, and your deeds, and observe the commandments of God, and continue in the faith of what ye have heard concerning the coming of our Lord, even unto the end of your lives, ye must perish. And now, O man, remember, and perish not" (Mosiah 4:29-30).

That, ultimately, is the nature of our search for happiness. It continues. It never ends. If anything, it becomes even more rewarding and fulfilling as we endure to the end and share our happiness with our families and loved ones and all mankind everywhere—on both sides of the veil.

THIS IS OUR DAY

This is our day. It is a time that has been foreseen by holy prophets since the world began. It is the dispensation of the fulness of times, when the final scenes of this planet's tumultuous history will be played out. Our latter-day prophets, from Joseph Smith to Gordon B. Hinckley, have warned us of the solemn, sobering obligation that is ours to prepare for "the great and dreadful day of the Lord" (D&C 2:1). That day is at hand, and there is still much to be done.

Said the Prophet Joseph Smith: "Brethren, shall we not go on in so great a cause? Go forward and not backward. Courage, brethren; and on, on to the victory! Let your hearts rejoice, and be exceedingly glad. Let the earth break forth into singing" (D&C 128:22).

Ours is a wonderful day in which to live. We have the fulness of the gospel of Jesus Christ. We are anchored by our faith in Him. We have daily opportunities to strengthen the links in the chains that hold us fast to that faith. We have the whisperings of the Holy Spirit to teach us of new links to work on. Like Marley's ghost—only in a positive affirmation of all that is good about this mortal experience—we can say, "I wear the chain I forged in life." Forge it strong, one link at a time.

"Therefore, continue your journey and let your hearts rejoice; for behold, and lo, I am with you even unto the end" (D&C 100:12).

Sources Cited

Ballard, Margaret McNeil. Family records in possession of author.

Ballard, Melvin J. *Sermons and Missionary Services of Melvin J. Ballard.* Comp. Bryant S. Hinckley. Salt Lake City: Deseret Book, 1949.

Ballard, Melvin R. *Melvin J. Ballard—Crusader for Righteousness.* Salt Lake City: Bookcraft, 1966.

Bartlett's Familiar Quotations. Comp. John Bartlett. Ed. Emily Morison Beck. Boston: Little, Brown, and Co., 1980.

Bennett, William J. "Redeeming Our Time." *Imprimis* 24, no. 11 (November 1995): 3.

Benson, Ezra Taft. *Ensign,* May 1980, 32.

Clayton, William. Letter of 10 December 1840 from Commerce, Illinois. William Clayton Collection. Archives of The Church of Jesus Christ of Latter-day Saints, Salt Lake City.

Covey, Stephen R. *The Divine Center.* Salt Lake City: Bookcraft, 1982.

Cowley, Matthias. *Wilford Woodruff: History of His Life and Labors.* Salt Lake City: Bookcraft, 1964.

Dickens, Charles. *A Christmas Carol.* London, 1843.

Evans, Richard L. Conference Report, October 1956, 101.

"The Family: A Proclamation to the World." *Ensign,* November 1995, 102.

Flake, Lawrence R. *George Q. Cannon: His Missionary Years.* Salt Lake City: Bookcraft, 1998.

Gibbons, Francis M. *Joseph F. Smith.* Salt Lake City: Deseret Book, 1984.

Grant, Heber J. Conference Report, October 1919, 7.

Hafen, LeRoy R., and Ann W. Hafen. *Handcarts to Zion: The Story of a Unique Western Migration, 1856-1860.* Glendale, Calif.: A. H. Clark, 1976.

Hamilton, Edith. *Mythology.* New York: New American Library, 1969.

Hinckley, Gordon B. *Ensign,* May 1991, 59.

——. *Ensign,* May 1995, 53, 87-88.

——. *Ensign,* May 1998, 88.

Hunter, Howard W. *Ensign,* November 1994, 88.

Huntington, Oliver B. Diary, 1842-74. Harold B. Lee Library, Brigham Young University, Provo, Utah.

Hymns of The Church of Jesus Christ of Latter-day Saints. Salt Lake City: The Church of Jesus Christ of Latter-day Saints, 1985.

Jessee, Dean C. *The Personal Writings of Joseph Smith.* Salt Lake City: Deseret Book, 1984.

Journal of Discourses. 26 vols. London: Latter-day Saints' Book Depot, 1854-86.

Kimball, Spencer W. *Faith Precedes the Miracle.* Salt Lake City: Deseret Book, 1973.

——. *My Beloved Sisters.* Salt Lake City: Deseret Book, 1979.

——. *Ensign,* October 1974, 5.

Kimball, Stanley B. *Mormon Pioneer National Historic Trail.* Historic Resource Study Series. Washington, D.C.: United States Department of the Interior, National Park Service, 1991.

Lee, Harold B. *Stand Ye in Holy Places.* Salt Lake City: Deseret Book, 1974.

McKay, David O. *Man May Know for Himself.* Comp. Clare Middlemiss. Salt Lake City: Deseret Book, 1967.

——. *Pathways to Happiness.* Comp. Llewelyn R. McKay. Salt Lake City: Deseret Book, 1957.

New Dictionary of Quotations on Historical Principles from Ancient and Modern Sources. Sel. H. L. Mencken. New York: Alfred A. Knopf, 1942.

Nibley, Charles W. "Reminiscences." In Joseph F. Smith, *Gospel Doctrine,* Salt Lake City: Deseret Book, 1939.

Nielson, Jens. Journal. Quoted in *Wyoming Trails Resource Handbook,* Salt Lake City: The Church of Jesus Christ of Latter-day Saints, 1996.

Packer, Boyd K. *Ensign,* May 1987, 24.

Roberts, B. H. *The Life of John Taylor.* Salt Lake City: Bookcraft, 1963.

Romney, Marion G. *Ensign,* November 1982, 93.

Smith, Joseph. *History of The Church of Jesus Christ of Latter-day Saints.* Ed. B. H. Roberts. 2d ed. rev., 7 vols. Salt Lake City: The Church of Jesus Christ of Latter-day Saints, 1931-52.

——. *Teachings of the Prophet Joseph Smith.* Sel. Joseph Fielding Smith. Salt Lake City: Deseret Book, 1976.

Smith, Joseph F. *Gospel Doctrine.* Salt Lake City: Deseret Book, 1939.

———. Conference Report, April 1917, 4.

Snow, LeRoi C. "How Lorenzo Snow Found God." *Improvement Era,* February 1937, 82–84, 105.

Stapley, Delbert L. Conference Report, April 1957, 77.

Talmage, James E. *Jesus the Christ.* 3d ed. Salt Lake City: The Church of Jesus Christ of Latter-day Saints, 1924.

Tanner, John. "Sketch of an Elder's Life." *Scraps of Biography.* Vol. 10 of the Faith-Promoting Series. Salt Lake City: Juvenile Instructor Office, 1883.

Taylor, John. *Millennial Star* 9 (1 November 1846): 321.

Thomson, Lord [Ray Herbert]. *After I Was Sixty.* London: Hamish Hamilton, 1975.

Tullidge, Edward W. *The Women of Mormondom.* New York, 1877. Reprint, Salt Lake City, 1975.

Whitney, Orson F. *The Life of Heber C. Kimball.* 5th ed. Salt Lake City: Bookcraft, 1974.

Wilcox, Ella Wheeler. "The Winds of Fate."

Woodruff, Wilford. *Discourses of Wilford Woodruff.* Salt Lake City: Bookcraft, 1946.

———. Conference Report, April 1898, 57.

Young, Emily D. P. "Autobiography." *Woman's Exponent* 13 (1884): 138.

INDEX